The Compre
to i

© 2019 iTandCoffee

iOS 12 / Mac OS Mojave Edition

All rights reserved. No part of this book shall be reproduced, stored in a retrieval system or transmitted by any means, electronic, mechanical, photocopying, recording, or otherwise without written permission from iTandCoffee.

No patent liability is assumed with respect to the use of the information contained herein.

Although every precaution has been taken in the preparation of this book, the author assumes no responsibility for any errors or omissions.

Nor is any liability assumed for damages resulting from the use of the information contained herein.

Special Sales and Supply Queries

For any information about buying this title in bulk quantities, or for supply of this title for educational or fund-raising purposes, contact iTandCoffee on **1300 885 420** or email **enquiry@itandcoffee.com.au**.

Who is iTandCoffee?

iTandCoffee is based in Melbourne, Australia, and offers technology education and support that focuses on empowering others to safely use and enjoy their technology.

Visit **www.itandcoffee.com.au** for more information and all sorts of useful online content.

iTandCoffee classes and private appointments

For queries about classes and private appointments with iTandCoffee, call 1300 885 420 or email **enquiry@itandcoffee.com.au**.

The Comprehensive Guide to iCloud

TABLE OF CONTENTS

INTRODUCTION THE MYSTERY THAT IS ICLOUD! — 10

FIRST, LET'S TALK ABOUT *THE CLOUD* — 11
- What is The Cloud — 11
- How many clouds are there? — 12
- My Clouds follow me wherever I go! — 13
- Do my clouds share my data? — 13
- What distinguishes my cloud from other people's clouds? — 14
- Do my cloud accounts share my email password? — 14

SO, WHAT IS ICLOUD? — 15
- What does iCloud do? — 15
- What does 'synchronise' mean? — 16
- When does syncing occur? — 16
- Syncing used to be done using iTunes — 16

SHOULD YOU USE ICLOUD? — 18

HOW BIG IS YOUR ICLOUD? — 19
- How much storage does Apple give you? — 19
- If you need more than 5GB — 19
- Backups and iCloud Photos can easily blow your free limit — 20

CONNECTING YOUR DEVICE TO 'ICLOUD' — 22
- You need your very own iCloud – it's not for sharing! — 22
- Does your iCloud Apple ID need to match that for iTunes? — 22
- The consequences of a shared iCloud Apple ID — 23
- How do I check whether I am using iCloud? — 24
- Connecting to your iCloud on your existing device — 25
- If you don't have your own Apple ID — 26

SETTING UP ICLOUD ON A NEW IOS DEVICE — 27
- Restoring from an iCloud Backup — 27
- Set Up as New iPhone — 28

The Comprehensive Guide to iCloud

TABLE OF CONTENTS

SETTING UP ICLOUD ON A MAC	**29**
Set up iCloud for existing Mac User	29
Setting up iCloud for new Mac User	29
Beware of the Desktop and Documents in iCloud option	29
Finishing off iCloud setup on Mac	30
SETTING UP ICLOUD ON WINDOWS	**31**
CREATING A NEW APPLE ID	**32**
YOUR ICLOUD SETTINGS	**34**
Viewing your iCloud settings	34
iCloud Storage Summary	34
Choose whether to sync key app data using iCloud	35
Why you might not use iCloud to sync Contacts, Calendars, Notes, etc.	35
Photos in iCloud	36
Should the Mail option be On or Off?	37
Other key sync options	38
Find my iPhone (or iPad, Mac)	39
iCloud Backup (iOS Only)	40
iCloud Drive	40
The last two options (iOS Only)	41
Some things that don't sync to iCloud	42
Your iCloud for Windows Settings	42
BACKING UP IOS DEVICES TO ICLOUD	**44**
Why do a backup?	44
Two options for iOS device backups	44
You can still back up to iTunes	44
Choosing to back up to iCloud	45
When does the iCloud Backup occur?	45
Viewing details of your iCloud Backups	46
A full list of what does and doesn't back up to iCloud	47

The Comprehensive Guide to iCloud

TABLE OF CONTENTS

ALL ABOUT ICLOUD DRIVE — **48**
- What is iCloud Drive — 48
- App Data in iCloud — 48
- Files and Folders in iCloud Drive — 49
- Accessing iCloud Drive's folders and files on Mac — 50
- Accessing iCloud Drive's folders and files on iOS — 50
- Preventing iCloud Drive from using Mobile Data — 51

"MY ICLOUD IS FULL — WHAT CAN I DO?" — **52**
- Options for reducing iCloud storage. — 52
- Do you store your Photos library in iCloud? — 53
- Do you have excess iOS backups in iCloud? — 54
- Are there iOS apps that don't need to back up? — 55
- Are unnecessary apps syncing data using iCloud? — 56
- What apps are using the most iCloud storage? — 57
- Deleting App Data from iCloud — 58
- Are files and folders using up space? — 59

MOVING DESKTOP & DOCUMENTS OUT OF ICLOUD — **60**
- Are your Mac's Desktop & Documents folders stored in iCloud? — 60

GETTING ADDITIONAL ICLOUD STORAGE — **63**

MANAGING YOUR ICLOUD DRIVE FILES ON IOS — **65**
- Introducing the Files App — 65
- Creating Folders & Sub-Folders in iCloud Drive — 67
- Moving Items between Folders in iCloud Drive — 67
- Delete files or folders in iCloud Drive — 68
- Recovering Deleted items in iCloud Drive — 69

ACCESSING YOUR ICLOUD FROM ANY COMPUTER — **70**
- Your iCloud accessible from any computer — 70
- View and manage Photos in iCloud — 71
- Pages, Keynote, Numbers editing from a Web Browser — 71
- Manage iCloud Drive content — 71
- Recover deleted iCloud Drive files — 71

The Comprehensive Guide to iCloud

TABLE OF CONTENTS

Find a lost device	71
Manage Contacts	71
Recover Contacts, Calendar, Reminders, Bookmarks	72
Set up 'Out of Office' reply for iCloud mail	72
Set up rules for your iCloud email	72
ENSURING THE SECURITY OF YOUR ICLOUD	**73**
Use a Strong, Different Password	73
Two-step verification	73
Two-Factor-Authentication	73
Setting up Two-Factor-Authentication	74
iCloud sign ins on older devices	75
MANAGING YOUR APPLE ID FROM A WEB BROWSER	**76**
appleid.apple.com	76
Changing the email address of your iCloud account	77
iforgot.apple.com	78
WHEN YOU FORGET YOUR APPLE PASSWORD	**79**
Change your Apple account's password using your iOS device's Passcode	79
What are the rules for Apple passwords?	80
Change your Apple ID's password from your Mac	80
If you don't have these password reset options	81
Resetting your password using iforgot.apple.com	82
FAMILY SHARING	**85**
Introducing Family Sharing	85
Setting up Family Sharing	85
Sharing iCloud Storage with the Family	87
Sharing your Location with your Family	87
Adjusting your Family Sharing settings	87
PHOTOS IN ICLOUD	**88**

The Comprehensive Guide to iCloud

TABLE OF CONTENTS

ICLOUD PHOTOS — 90
- Your iCloud Photos Options — 90
- The great benefits of iCloud Photos — 90
- The disadvantages of iCloud Photos — 91
- Photos on the Mac says there are no photos to import — 92
- Should you use iCloud Photos? — 92
- Turning off iCloud Photos — 93

GETTING YOUR PHOTOS OUT OF ICLOUD PHOTOS — 94
- See your iCloud Photos in icloud.com — 94
- Download a selection of photos from iCloud.com — 94
- Download originals or edited versions — 95
- Where do the downloaded photos go? — 95
- If you choose to download a large number of photos — 96
- Temporarily turn on iCloud Photos on a Mac — 96
- Before you turn on iCloud Photos on a Mac … — 97
- Getting your Photos out of iCloud Photos – Windows — 99

MY PHOTO STREAM — 101

SHARED ALBUMS — 102
- Share photos with friends and family — 102
- Enabling Shared Albums — 102

SOLVING ICLOUD CONFUSION — 103
- Before you sign out — 103
- How to sign out of the wrong iCloud — 104
- If you were using a shared iTunes account — 105
- Other sign outs may be required – Messages & Facetime — 105

Introduction
The mystery that is iCloud!

iCloud is big mystery to many users of Apple devices. Many people steer clear of using it, and families can easily find themselves in a quite a mess when they initially set up iCloud on various devices, using their existing Apple ID that they use for iTunes and App Store purchases.

It is important to understand what iCloud is, and what it does, <u>before</u> you start using it - so that you can properly take advantage of the features it offers - and avoid such a mess.

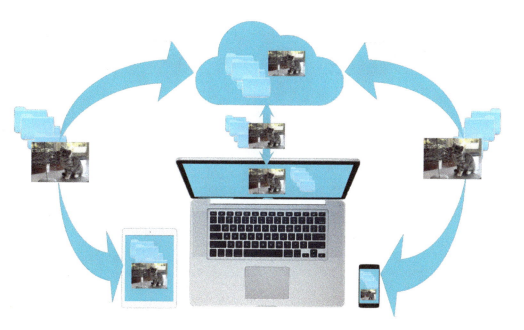

iCloud provides something called **cloud storage** for some (not all) information on your Apple device/s.

Its main purpose is to make your important information – things like Contacts, Calendars, Notes, Pictures, files and app data - available across all your Apple devices (and Windows too), without you having to enter information more than once and copy between devices. It is also designed to keep your information safe, through its backup service.

Before we talk more about iCloud, let's look at what we mean when we talk about *the cloud*.

First, let's talk about *The Cloud*

What is The Cloud

You may have heard the terms **The Cloud** or **Cloud Storage**.

You may have thought that this meant the same thing as **iCloud**.

Cloud Storage means that your data is stored on a data storage computer (called a **file server**) somewhere in the world.

In the case of iCloud, your data is stored on a file server owned and operated by Apple in one of their massive data centres. An example of a building housing a data centre is shown below.

Image by Tom Rafferty at https://www.flickr.com/photos/67945918@N00/5596941479

Your data is transferred to and from the data centre using the internet.

Just picture a space on one of the below banks of computers, that has your very own Apple ID (your email address) recorded on it, and where all your iCloud information is securely stored - protected by your password and, hopefully, another layer of protection called **two-factor-authentication** (which we cover from page 73).

First, let's talk about *The Cloud*

Your Cloud storage is like your very own safety deposit box at the bank, for which only you have the key.

But you don't have to travel to the bank to access the contents of this safety deposit box – you can access it from your computer or mobile device from anywhere in the world, as long as you have access to the internet and have the key (your email address and password).

How many clouds are there?

As mentioned earlier, many people I see think that iCloud is **THE** cloud - that **iCloud** and **The Cloud** mean the same thing.

This is not the case. Apple's iCloud is just one of many cloud services.

Other Cloud Storage services are offered by companies like Microsoft, Google, Dropbox, Evernote, and other businesses worldwide.

In my case, I utilise several Cloud services for sharing and synchronising data between my various devices. This allows me to ensure that I have access to all sorts of information, no matter which device I am using.

The below illustration gives a visual representation of the cloud services I use on all my devices.

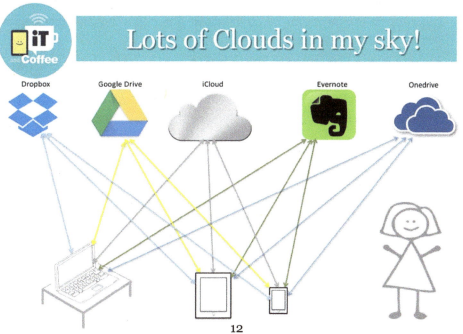

First, let's talk about *The Cloud*

My Clouds follow me wherever I go!

I like to picture that I have several different shaped clouds floating above my head, going with me wherever I go – something like the picture shown on the previous page!

The arrows represent the two-way flow of data between my different cloud services and my iPad, iPhone, Macbook and Windows computer.

As you can see in the picture on the previous page, I have my iCloud cloud, but I also have

- My **Dropbox** cloud - which I use to share selected files between my computer and all my other devices. I mainly use Dropbox for sharing folders and files with other people, as my main cloud storage is in OneDrive. (I use the free version of Dropbox, so have limited storage – but have a large amount of storage in OneDrive.)
- My **Google Drive** cloud - which stores some other files that are linked to my Google / Gmail account – questionnaires and surveys that I use for business purposes.
- My **Evernote** cloud - which I use to store all sorts of notes, articles, bills, school notices, receipts, and much more. It is like a digital scrapbook where I can put all sorts of things, and then easily search for them and view them. I can even set reminders on Evernote notes! I pay an annual subscription to use advanced features of Evernote.
- My **OneDrive** cloud - which stores all my business and personal files. I have created a folder/sub-folder structure in my OneDrive that helps me find what I need. I then share certain folders with other members of the iTandCoffee Team, so that we are looking at and managing the same set of files and folders.

Do my clouds share my data?

The different brands of cloud services do not talk to each other – they are quite separate.

I have installed apps on each of my devices to set up the connections with each of my cloud service (by signing in with my email address and password for that service) and to enable syncing and accessing of the data stored there.

First, let's talk about *The Cloud*

What distinguishes my cloud from other people's clouds?

For each of my cloud services, I use my **email address** to identify the account that I hold with that Cloud service provider. This is often the same email address across each cloud service and provides me with a unique login to that particular service – since no-one else has the same email address as me!

I also make sure I use a **different, strong password** for each of these accounts.

This is a security precaution - just in case someone manages to find out my account ID and password for one of my other online accounts. If I use the same email address and password combination for each, then I may be giving them unauthorized access to my other accounts – and to my valuable data.

Do my cloud accounts share my email password?

The fact that you use your email address to identify your account with each of these cloud services can cause confusion for many people.

As mentioned just above, the reason you use an email address is so that you can be uniquely identified – since no one else in the world can have the same email address.

Using your email address to identify your account also allows the Cloud service provider to easily email you whenever required.

So, the account you set up with one provider is entirely separate from that you set up with another provider – even though you may use the same email address for each.

As already mentioned, it is good practice to ALWAYS use different passwords for the different online accounts that you set up.

This can protect you in the situation where you inadvertently give away a particular password, or where one of your online services is perhaps hacked and password credentials stolen – something that has happened previously to sites like Adobe, LinkedIn, Yahoo and others.

So, what is iCloud?

iCloud is the cloud service offered by Apple, a service that works on iPads, iPhones, iPod Touches, Apple TV's, Macs and Windows computers.

What does iCloud do?

On any iCloud-enabled device, you can choose to

- Synchronise certain data between devices – your Contacts, Calendar, Reminders, Notes and more;
- Use an iCloud email address to manage your mail;
- Share your photos between your devices and with other people;
- Store and share your entire photo library if you so desire;
- Synchronise App data between your Apple devices;
- Store your files and sync them between your devices (including your Mac or Windows computer);
- See the same set of bookmarks for your web browsing across devices;
- Store your Messages and sync them between Apple devices;
- Share passwords between Apple devices;
- Back up your iPad and iPhone data;
- Find your iPhone/iPad/Mac if you lose it (and lock others out if it is stolen).

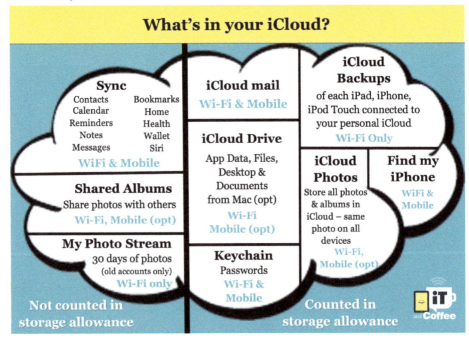

So, what is iCloud?

Each of these iCloud features is optional – you choose which to turn on or off on each of your devices through that device's settings/preferences.

These different aspects of iCloud make it quite different to a lot of other cloud storage services, which don't necessarily provide the same level of service and synchronisation.

Picture your iCloud as having various parts to it (see image on previous page) – and you choose which parts of this cloud you want to use, and don't want to use.

What does 'synchronise' mean?

If you have multiple devices, synchronising means that data and files created, entered or changed on one device will appear or update on your other devices as well, as long as all devices are signed in to the same iCloud account.

This syncing will happen automatically when you are connected to the internet.

As an example, when you add a Contact on your iPhone, you may find it magically appears on your iPad as well. This is due to synchronising – shortened to **syncing**.

When does syncing occur?

Many things in your iCloud will sync over 3G/4G (i.e. cellular/mobile data) <u>AND</u> Wi-Fi.

Other types of data in iCloud will only sync over Wi-Fi – mainly because of the amount of data that could be involved in syncing.

For some types of data, you can choose whether or not syncing occurs when you are on mobile data – so that you can avoid excess data usage on your iPhone's data plan (or your data plan on your iPad, if you have one).

This is generally done from your Settings app, from the item in Settings for that App (or from Settings -> Mobile, which is sometimes Mobile Data, Cellular or Cellular Data).

Syncing used to be done using iTunes

In the days before iCloud, the only way to keep your devices showing the same information was to 'sync' the devices using iTunes on a computer.

So, what is iCloud?

With the introduction of iCloud, you no longer need to have a computer to achieve this synchronisation. (Although, you can still sync and backup to iTunes as well if you like.)

With iCloud, you no longer need to have a laptop or desktop computer in your life at all!

The iPad (and iPhone) can do nearly everything a computer can do – and certainly can do everything that the majority of users need.

Should you use iCloud?

It is your choice whether you use iCloud. Many people feel uncomfortable about setting up an internet-based account.

The reality is that most people already have at least one internet-based account. I hear Gmail email users tell my they don't trust iCloud – and they are surprised when I explain that their Gmail account is also a 'cloud'.

If you choose not to use iCloud, you need to think about whether your device has anything of value on it that you would be sorry to lose.

If anything happened to the device (i.e. if it is lost, stolen, broken or you forget your passcode), you may lose important information like your contacts, diary, Notes and, most importantly, your photos.

If you have a computer, you may choose to sync and back-up your iPad/iPhone using the computer instead of iCloud.

This is done using the iTunes app on your computer.

If you choose this option, you need to ensure that such a backup is done very regularly if you have any data you value on your device.

If you don't own a computer, you definitely should consider using iCloud.

I regularly hear clients tell me that they don't 'trust' iCloud – usually based on something they heard in the press or because of mistrust by another family member.

Ensuring the security of any online information is all about selecting a good, strong password and ensuring you don't ever give away this password.

To me, it is also essential to add an additional security precaution for any online account, to ensure that your data is never accessed without your permission. This is called Two-Factor Authentication.

We'll talk about this in relation to iCloud from page 73.

How big is your iCloud?

How much storage does Apple give you?

Apple gives you **5GB of free storage** in your iCloud.

To give you an idea of just what you can fit into 5GB of storage, here is one of iTandCoffee's handy charts.

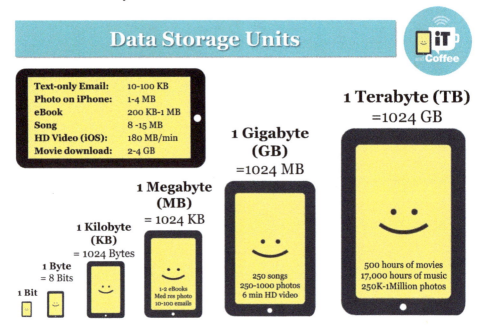

If you need more than 5GB

Additional iCloud data can be easily purchased if you need more – and this can be done on your iPhone, iPad, Mac or Windows computer. Here are the options and costs for upgrading your iCloud storage (in Australia $).

How big is your iCloud?

The good news is that the standard information that you sync using iCloud *does not count* towards the free 5GB. Here is that diagram again - all items on the left side of the thick vertical bar are not counted towards your free allowance.

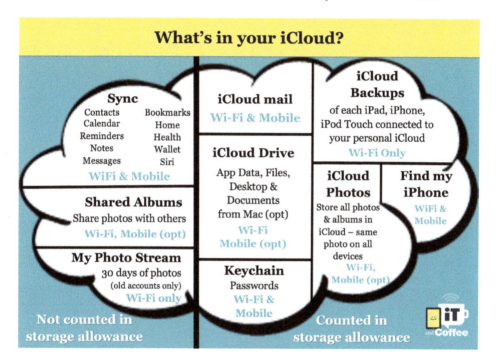

Even your **My Photo Stream** and **Shared Album** storage (described from page 88) is provided in addition to the 5GB.

So, you really get far more than 5GB for free.

For many people who only use iCloud for keeping their data 'in sync', there may never by any need to purchase additional storage from Apple.

Backups and iCloud Photos can easily blow your free limit

Backups of your iPad and iPhone can use up a lot of data, especially if you have a lot of photos and videos, or a large set of POP email account Mailboxes. (We will cover more about what 'backing up' means from page 44.)

How big is your iCloud?

If you do choose to back up your device/s to iCloud, you may find that your free 5GB runs out pretty quickly.

If you have turned on a feature called iCloud Photos, your iCloud may quickly fill up with thousands of photos.

If you find you need more space, this can be purchased from Apple very easily.

If you upgrade to the 200GB or 2TB iCloud plans, you can share your storage with other members of your family. We cover this from page 87.

We'll cover the topic of iCloud backups from page 44, and how to get more storage from page 63.

Connecting your device to 'iCloud'

You need your very own iCloud – it's not for sharing! [1]

iCloud allows you to connect all of <u>your own</u> devices to the same 'iCloud' account.

Do not use the same Apple ID to sign into iCloud on anyone else's device – especially your child's device. They must have their own Apple ID.

Do not sign in to your own device/s using another person's Apple ID or a shared 'family' iTunes Apple ID.

Here is another illustration showing that different people need different iClouds to manage and sync their own data.

Does your iCloud Apple ID need to match that for iTunes?

It is OK for your iCloud Apple ID to be a different Apple ID to that which you use for the **iTunes and App Store**.

Multiple people can use the same **iTunes and App Store Apple ID** (to save purchasing the same App or other content more than once), but the same should not apply for your iCloud ID.

---

[1] This is a general rule – there may be some cases where iCloud is, in fact, set up to be shared by two or more people. However, this not a standard practice and is not recommended.

Connecting your device to 'iCloud'

In saying that, these days it is usually better to set up iCloud's 'Family Sharing' for managing family purchases and have each family member using their own Apple ID for iTunes and App Store purchases. More on this from page 85.

The consequences of a shared iCloud Apple ID

I have come across far too many situations where valuable data (for example Contacts, Photos, Notes) have been mistakenly deleted due to a shared iCloud Apple ID and what I call 'iCloud Confusion'.

This has occurred when an existing iCloud Apple ID has been used on another person's iPad or iPhone, and where that other person has decided they don't need the set of Contacts that they have 'inherited' from the first person – and so deletes them all!

Oops – there go all the Contacts belonging to the person who 'owns' the iCloud Apple ID. *(Note. These days, Contacts can by more easily restored by visiting iCloud.com from a web browser – more on this from page 70.)*

I have also seen disharmony and even breakups over Messages that have gone to the wrong family member or a friend's family member – caused by more than one person using the same Apple ID for iMessages.

Other consequences of a shared iCloud Apple ID can be (depending on the settings on each device):

- Calendars, Contacts, Notes, Reminders from all devices are merged and can be inadvertently deleted.
- Private passwords can be shared with others who use the same Apple ID.
- Phone call history is shared with others
- Others can track your location
- Several devices are using the same iCloud storage, resulting in a full iCloud.
- Family members may get each other's Messages
- Facetime calls may be received on wrong device/s.
- Photos end up merged – or even inadvertently deleted.
- Safari Bookmarks are from several people's 'favourites'

So, if you share an Apple ID with someone else for **iTunes and App Store** purchases, you (or they) will need to choose a different Apple ID to use for iCloud, iMessage and Facetime. We cover what to do in this scenario in the last section of this guide, from page 103.

Connecting your device to 'iClo

How do I check whether I am using iCloud?

On the iPad and iPhone

On your iPad and iPhone, go to your **Settings** app.

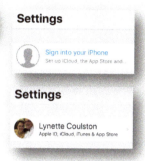

If you see a message like that on the top right (showing that you need to sign in), then you are not currently using iCloud on this device.

If this area shows your name, then you are currently signed in to an iCloud account on that iPhone or iPad.

On the Mac

On your Mac, visit your -> **System Preferences**, and choose the **iCloud** option.

If you see a screen like that below left, your Mac is not currently signed in to iCloud. If it looks something like that below right, you are signed in to iCloud.

Connecting your device to 'iCloud'

On Windows

On Windows, you must have downloaded and installed **iCloud for Windows** and, as part of that installation process, have signed in to iCloud.

You can check if you have iCloud on your Windows computer by checking you have the **iCloud Desktop app** in the Start menu, or by using Cortana's search (as shown on right) to find it.

If you don't have iCloud Desktop app on your computer, or if you click on it and it shows the below screen, then your Windows computer is not currently connected to iCloud.

The Desktop app will show your iCloud details if your Windows computer is already connected to iCloud (see above right)

Connecting to your iCloud on your existing device

You connect to iCloud in your **Settings** app on each iPad and iPhone, in your **System Preferences** on your Mac, and from your **iCloud for Windows** app on a Windows computer.

Choose the Sign In option that appears on your device.

Sign in with your iCloud Apple ID (i.e. the email address you used to set up your iCloud) and the corresponding password.

Connecting your device to 'iCloud'

If you have forgotten your account's password, choose the option **Don't have an Apple ID or forgot it?** on the iPhone/iPad, or **Forgot Apple ID or password?** on Mac and Windows, and follow the prompts to reset your password.

(We discuss what to do about a forgotten Apple ID password from page 79.)

Depending on your iCloud security settings – and whether you have any other Apple devices – you may then see a message pop up on another device's screen, advising that someone is trying to access your account.

Even if the location is not quite where you are currently located (!), choose the **Allow** option and then enter the 6-digit verification code provided.

If you don't have your own Apple ID

If you don't have an Apple ID of your very own, it is very easy to create a free one for use by iCloud. We look at on page 32.

Setting up iCloud on a new iOS Device

For new iOS devices, setting up iCloud (or connecting to an existing iCloud account) is done as part of the initial set up steps for the device.

You will have several options for initial setup of a device

- **Restore from iCloud Backup** for an iPad or iPhone if you have previously backed up a device to iCloud.
- **Restore from iTunes Backup** if you have backed up your previous device to iTunes on a computer and want to use this backup to set up your new device.
- **Set Up as New iPhone** if you are new to iPhone or know that you don't have an iCloud or iTunes backup.
- **Move Data from Android** if you have previously used an Android device

In this guide we will only look at the first and third options above.

Restoring from an iCloud Backup

If you choose **Restore from iCloud Backup**, the sign in screen on right will appear.

Sign in with your Apple ID (i.e. the email address) and its password.

You will be presented with the details of the latest backup that can be found in iCloud for that Apple ID.

Choose the backup that applies, and follow the prompts to complete the restoration and setup of your device.

Make sure that you stay connected to Wi-Fi and have sufficient battery charge for the duration of this restore/setup. Ideally, put your device on a charger.

27

Setting up iCloud on a new iOS Device

Set Up as New iPhone

If you already have an iCloud Apple ID

Sign in with your iCloud account's email address and password to enable your iCloud.

If you have a different Apple ID for iTunes and iCloud, you can instead choose the **Use different Apple IDs for iCloud and iTunes?** option at the bottom of the sign in screen.

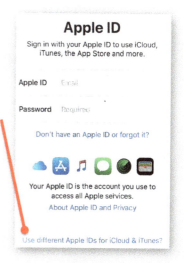

This allows you to sign in first with your iCloud Apple ID, then sign in to iTunes and App Store with your iTunes Apple ID.

If you don't have an Apple ID

If you don't have your own Apple ID, or have forgotten your iCloud account's password, choose **Don't have an Apple ID OR forgot it?** to get the screen on the right.

Choose **Create a Free Apple ID if** you need to create a new account.

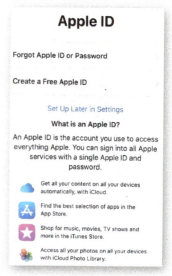

We'll cover the steps involved in setting up this new Apple ID from page 32.

Setting up iCloud on a Mac

Setting up iCloud on your Mac is very similar to your iPad and iPhone.

Set up iCloud for existing Mac User

If you are already set up on your Mac, choose **the System Preferences** app from the dock, or go to -> **System Preferences** and choose the **iCloud** option.

Sign in with your Apple ID and Password (or choose **Create Apple ID** to create a new iCloud account – which we cover on page 32).

Setting up iCloud for new Mac User

If you are setting up your Mac for the first time (or logging into a new user account for the first time), you will be prompted to enter your iCloud Apple ID as part of this setup.

Beware of the Desktop and Documents in iCloud option

Once you have entered these details, you may be asked if you wish to **Store files from Documents and Desktop in iCloud Drive**.

Only tick this option if you wish to store all files from the Desktop & Documents folders in iCloud.

This will mean that this content would then be available on all other devices that are signed in to the same iCloud.

If you have a lot of files, you may need to purchase additional iCloud storage to accommodate your files and folders from your Desktop and Documents area.

Only enable this option if you definitely want to use iCloud to store these folders.

Setting up iCloud on a Mac

Finishing off iCloud setup on Mac

You will be asked if you wish to use iCloud for all your documents and data, and for **Find My Mac**.

Generally, you will leave both of these ticked and choose **Next**.

(Note. The reference to documents and data here is not referring to your Desktop and Documents area – this is an option that is separately selected.)

Alternatively, leave these options un-ticked at this point and manually turn on/off your iCloud features once your Mac is signed in to your account.

Then answer whatever prompts you see, to complete your setup.

If your Apple ID has something called two-factor authentication enabled, you will need to authorize the sign in using a password that applied on your computer, or from another authorized device. We'll cover two-factor authentication later in the guide (page 73).

Setting up iCloud on Windows

iCloud can be installed on a Windows computer, allowing you to access many of the key services provided by Apple's iCloud.

If you have not yet installed iCloud for Windows, go to

https://support.apple.com/en-au/HT204283

and choose **Download**.

Install the **iCloud** app by following the prompts. You will need to restart your computer after the installation completes.

On restart you should be presented with the iCloud sign in screen. Sign in to your iCloud from here. To get to this screen otherwise, go to your **Start** menu and choose **iCloud Desktop app** (or, if it is visible in the Start menu, type **iCloud** into Cortana's search bar to find this iCloud app.

You will then be presented with a similar screen to that which applies on Mac and iOS devices allowing you to choose what features of iCloud you would like to use (see below).

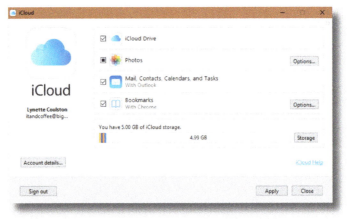

More on these **iCloud for Windows** settings from page 42.

Creating a new Apple ID

As mentioned earlier, if you don't yet have an Apple ID, just choose the **Don't have an Apple ID or forgot it?** option on the iPad/iPhone or the **Create New Apple ID** option on the Mac.

(You cannot create a new Apple ID from a Windows computer.)

Tap **Get a Free Apple ID** option on the iPad/iPhone.

On both the iPad/iPhone and Mac, you will then need to enter your birthdate to get started.

When creating a new Apple ID, you can use an email address that you already own (but, once again, make sure it is yours and yours alone).

As an example, you could use your *gmail.com* or *outlook.com* email address.

It is best to avoid using a school or work email address, and these are subject to change.

Instead of using an existing email address, you can choose to create a brand-new Apple iCloud email address which will have the format *yourname@icloud.com*.

You will just need to choose a *yourname* name that has not been used by any other **@icloud.com** user in the world – sometimes a challenge, especially for more common names!

If you choose to create an Apple email address, this email address can be used just as your iCloud & iTunes account id or, optionally, as an email address that you use for emails (in the Mail app).

Creating a new Apple ID

If you don't need another email address, you will be able to choose to 'turn off' its use by the Mail app. However, it will always be available to you should you want to use it in future.

When creating this new Apple ID, follow the prompts that are presented, filling in and answering all the questions that are provided – including a mobile number that is associated with the Apple ID.

You will need to select a password – one that is at least 8 characters, has at least one upper and lower-case letter and at least one number. You may not be allowed to use just a word or name and number, as this will be deemed too simple.

If you use an email address that you already own, you will be sent an email to that address.

You will need to find the email that Apple sends you (perhaps on another device if you are setting up a new device) and follow the instructions to confirm that you own the email address.

This confirmation involves clicking/tapping the link in the email you just received and signing in with your new Apple ID and password.

Your iCloud Settings

Viewing your iCloud settings

You can see your current set of iCloud settings by visiting

- **Settings -> [your-name] -> iCloud** on an iOS device
- ** -> System Preferences -> iCloud** on a Mac
- **iCloud Desktop app** on a Windows computer (from the **Start** menu)

While the settings you see will differ on the different devices, we will focus on iOS Devices first and cover the Mac-specific and iCloud for Windows settings towards the end of this section.

iCloud Storage Summary

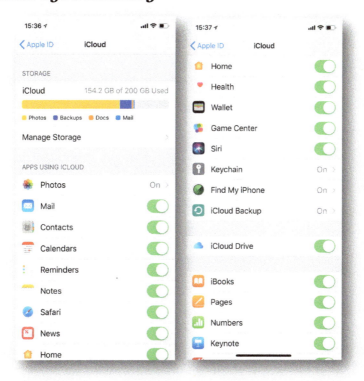

The first section of your iCloud settings on iOS shows the amount of storage you have used in your iCloud, and what that storage has been used for. (We'll talk more about managing iCloud Storage from page 52.)

(On the Mac and Windows screens, the storage usage is shown along the bottom.)

Your iCloud Settings

Choose whether to sync key app data using iCloud

The next section shows the set of standard apps that use iCloud.

The main data that the majority of users are concerned about when it comes to syncing is from:

      Contacts   **Calendars**   **Reminders**   **Notes**

(We'll talk about Photos and Mail settings shortly.)

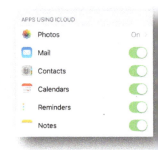

If you want to sync the data for these apps using your iCloud, turn on each of those settings.

You will be asked if you wish to merge any existing data of that type that has been, to date, just stored on your device.

It is best to answer **Yes** to this question to ensure that this data is added to your iCloud.

If you inadvertently end up with duplicates, these can be relatively easily sorted out later.

Why you might not use iCloud to sync Contacts, Calendars, Notes, etc.

The thing is, you don't HAVE to use iCloud to sync your Contacts, Calendars, Reminders and Notes data.

You may already be using another mail account that can sync this information between your devices – for example, your Gmail, Yahoo, Hotmail, Outlook or Exchange account.

Before switching on iCloud's syncing of this information, consider what other mail accounts you use and check their settings.

Visit **Settings -> Passwords Accounts** and tap on each account you see here to determine if they have the same set of options, and whether these are turned on or off.

As an example, above right is my Exchange account and its settings – showing that I am already using that account to sync some of the same data.

Your iCloud Settings

I use my Exchange email account for my work Contacts, Calendars and Reminders, but also have my personal set of Contacts, Calendars and Reminders that I store in iCloud– so I choose to turn on iCloud syncing of these details as well.

I choose to just use iCloud for syncing my Notes. I don't store Notes in my Exchange account, so have turned off this option in the Exchange account settings.

If you do choose to have more than one email account syncing a particular type of data, you will need to make sure you nominate which account is the **Default Account** that you wish to use when creating a new item of that type. This needs to be done on each of your devices, to ensure that are all putting new things in the correct account.

On your iPad and iPhone this is done in

- **Settings -> Contacts**,
- **Settings -> Calendars**,
- **Settings -> Reminders**
- **Settings -> Notes**

(On the Mac, visit the **Preferences** option for the relevant app to establish the **Default Account** setting for each. On Windows, your Outlook app – if you have it - controls these preferences.)

Photos in iCloud

As mentioned above, I skipped over the first option in that second section of iCloud settings – the **Photos** option. Tapping on it reveals the options shown at bottom right.

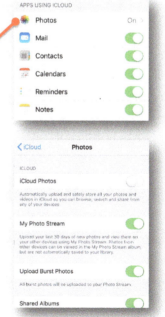

As this is a more complex area, requiring quite a lengthy discussion to cover the meaning of the various options you see there, we cover it in more detail later in this guide (page 88). One thing that I will say here though ...

DON'T TURN ON ICLOUD PHOTOS UNLESS YOU UNDERSTAND WHAT IT IS AND WHAT IT DOES!

Read the sections later in the document (from page 88) to understand this area before turning on this Apple service.

Your iCloud Settings

Should the Mail option be On or Off?

The answer to this question is: "It Depends".

If you have chosen to set up an Apple-provided email address for your iCloud (i.e. your-name@icloud.com or your-name@me.com), you can choose whether or not you want to use this Apple ID as an email account as well.

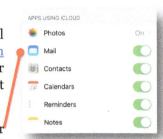

If you wish to enable sending and receiving mail for this Apple-provided email address, turn on the **Mail** option in iCloud settings.

If you have used your own (non-Apple) email address for iCloud, turning **On** the **Mail** option in iCloud may cause you some confusion!

Turning **On** iCloud Mail in this case does not mean that you are turning **On** that non-Apple email account in your Mail app.

If you haven't already added this non-Apple email account to your device, head to **Settings -> Passwords and Accounts** on iOS to do this.

On Mac, you add other email accounts in **Mail->Preferences->Accounts** or -> **Preferences -> Internet Accounts**.

(We won't cover how you do this on Windows, and it will depend on what Mail app you use there.)

If you turn on the **Mail** setting for iCloud for a non-Apple email address, you will be asked if you wish to create an Apple email account to associate with your iCloud account (if you haven't already done so).

To keep things simple in this introductory guide, just leave Mail set to **Off** if your email address is **not** one provided by Apple (unless you specifically do want to use an Apple email account that is associated with your iCloud account).

Your iCloud Settings

Other key sync options

Messages	Sync all your Messages to/from your iCloud.
Safari	Sync your Safari Favourites, other Bookmarks, Reading List and History across your devices
News, Home, Health, Wallet Stocks	Sync the data from these apps across all devices signed into iCloud
Siri	Sync your Siri and search settings (refer **Settings -> Siri & Search**) across devices.
Game Centre	Allows your Game Centre results (from apps that use Game Centre) to sync across devices.
Keychain	Sync your saved passwords across your devices. This syncs your **Keychain** on your Mac to iCloud. Sync'd iCloud can be viewed in the Mac app **Keychain Access**. On iOS devices, saved passwords are shown in **Settings->Passwords & Accounts-> Website & App Passwords**.

IMPORTANT NOTE ON KEYCHAIN:

Keychain is where all sorts of passwords may be saved - passwords for your mail accounts, Wi-Fi passwords, app passwords, passwords for website logins, and more.

Your Keychain will contain website login details from times when you agreed to save these details (by answering **Yes** to a question that popped up) in Safari. Saved login details (including passwords) can then autofill in Safari and other places.

Your passcode, fingerprint or Face (or, on a Mac, your Mac's password) is all that is required to access all the passwords that get stored in your Keychain.

Before turning on the Keychain option in iCloud settings, consider whether you have good passcode/password and whether anyone else has access to this passcode/password (or has a fingerprint stored on your device). If anyone else uses the same iCloud as you, they too could have access to all your passwords if you choose to sync your Keychain to iCloud.

Your iCloud Settings

Find my iPhone (or iPad, Mac)

You will also see a **Find my iPhone** (or **Find my iPad/Mac**) option in your iCloud Settings on iOS or Mac

This option is best **TURNED TO ON**, as it will help you to locate the device should it ever go missing – even if you have muted the device before it went missing!

In the worst-case scenario of the device being stolen, you will be able to perform a remote wipe of your device.

Additionally, by turning on **Find my ...**, you are will be locking your device so that, even if someone steals it and they wipe it, that person will not be able to activate the wiped device without knowing your iCloud password – thereby rendering the device useless to them.

This is a great theft deterrent introduced by Apple in recent years and has, reportedly, reduced the number of thefts of iPhones.

To ensure that you can find the last place your device was located before the battery died, make sure you also turn on the **Send Last Location** option.

To locate a lost device, you can sign into the **Find iPhone** app on another iOS Device; or visit **iCloud.com** on any computer, sign in with your Apple ID and password, and choose the **Find iPhone** option

All devices signed in to your iCloud will then be able to be viewed on a Map that shows the location of each.

For any device that you select, you can choose to

- Play a sound on it (even if it is muted),
- Put it into **Lost Mode** and leave a message on the screen, or
- Erase the device contents.

Your iCloud Settings

iCloud Backup (iOS Only)

Tap on this option to enable or disable **iCloud Backup** for your iOS device.

(Note. The iCloud Backup option is only available for your Apple mobile devices – not for your Mac. Mac's should be backed up using Time Machine.)

If the **iCloud Backup** option is on, your device will perform a backup to your iCloud on a regular basis – safely saving away any data on your device that would not otherwise be able to be retrieved if something disastrous happened to your device.

This backup can also be used to set up a brand-new device – so that you can 'pick up where you left off' with the old device.

We'll cover the topic of iCloud backups in more detail in a separate section, including what to do if your backup doesn't seem to work and how to manage what is backed up to iCloud.

For most people, I would suggest that it is a very good idea to turn iCloud Backup on.

iCloud Drive

Data associated with other apps other than the set described in the second section can by synced to your iCloud and other devices if you turn on the **iCloud Drive** option in iCloud settings.

Once you turn on the **iCloud Drive** option on the iPad and iPhone, you will see the list of apps on your device that are able to sync with iCloud using **iCloud Drive**.

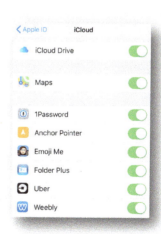

40

Your iCloud Settings

On the Mac, the **Options** button will appear when **iCloud Drive** is ticked – choose this to view the **iCloud Drive** settings on your Mac.

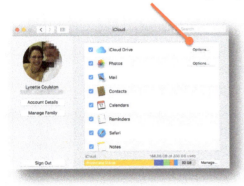 

Choose which of the listed apps should be able to store their data in **iCloud Drive** by turning on (or off) the switch on the right of that app (or ticking the item on the Mac).

If you see any apps in that list that don't need to be syncing data with other devices, you can turn off their switch – and save a bit of iCloud storage.

We cover iCloud Drive and storage in more detail later, from page 48.

The last two options (iOS Only)

Look Me Up — Certain apps can request access to look you up using your Apple ID. Visit this option to check if you have any such apps, and to turn off their access if desired.

Mail — This option is only relevant if you have an iCloud email address associated with your iCloud account. It shows your iCloud email address (plus any iCloud *alias* email addresses that exist for your iCloud account) and allows for the adjustment of these mail settings.

Your iCloud Settings

Some things that don't sync to iCloud

iCloud does not synchronise everything.

For example, iCloud will not sync your POP email account's emails (if you have this 'older' style of email account – one that does not synchronise between your devices) and will not sync app data that is not stored in iCloud. iCloud does not look after syncing of your IMAP or Exchange email account.

Another important thing to note is that, depending on your settings, iCloud may not be syncing ALL your photos and videos – even if you have turned on something called My Photo Stream. We cover more on this from page 88.

This is why it is important to use iCloud Backup to protect any data that could not be retrieved otherwise.

Your iCloud for Windows Settings

You don't see the full list of iCloud settings on a Windows computer. Visit your **iCloud** app (from the **Start** menu) to see the available options.

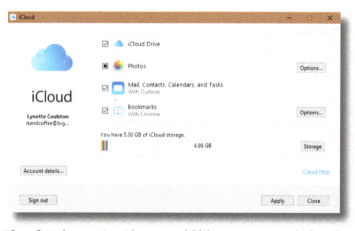

Tick the **iCloud Drive** option if you would like to sync your **iCloud Drive** files and folders to this computer.

If iCloud Drive is enabled, the **iCloud Drive** option will appear in your **File Explorer** under your **Quick Access** list. Your existing **iCloud Drive** files/folders (as found in iCloud) will show here, and anything new you put here will be uploaded to your **iCloud Drive** and shared with other devices that also have **iCloud Drive** enabled.

Your iCloud Settings

If you have included your **Desktop** and **Documents** folders from a Mac, these folders will be able to by viewed and managed from your Windows computer.

Click on the **Photos** option in your iCloud settings to see further options relating to what photos should sync with your Windows computer.

Choose whether you wish to use iCloud Photos, My Photo Stream and/or Shared Albums (which are all described later in this document, from page 88).

You will also see that you can choose where downloaded iCloud photos and videos are stored, where uploads to iCloud should be taken from, and where Shared Albums will be stored. Choose **Change** to adjust these location settings.

Your Quick Access list will include iCloud Photos, with separate folders for Download, Uploads and Shared.

If you have the Outlook app for managing your Mail, you will see the option to sync your **Mail, Contacts, Calendars and Tasks** with Outlook.

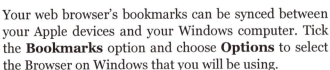

Your web browser's bookmarks can be synced between your Apple devices and your Windows computer. Tick the **Bookmarks** option and choose **Options** to select the Browser on Windows that you will be using.

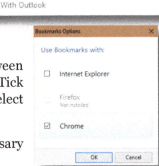

Follow the prompts (if they appear) to add the necessary **extension** to your browser to support this syncing.

Backing up iOS Devices to iCloud

Why do a backup?

Given that your iPhone and iPad are mobile devices that are carried around with you – and are therefore prone to damage, breakage or loss – it is a good idea to have an insurance policy to cover the data on your device in case of mishap.

This means ensuring that you have backed up any important data on your device, ideally so that – should you suffer an 'i-Disaster' – you can re-instate all your apps, data, settings and (usually most importantly) your photos onto a replacement device.

Two options for iOS device backups

Two options exist for backing up an iPad and iPhone. One involves the use of iTunes on a computer – plugging in your i-Device to a computer and, via iTunes, backing up the device to that computer.

This option will provide you with a full backup of your device and its contents. It is well worth doing this type of backup on a regular basis if you own a computer.

However, these days our mobile devices can carry a LOT of data – for example, my iPhone is a 256GB model. My Macbook only has 500GB of storage, so regular backups of my iPhone would use up far too much of my available Macbook storage.

In general, backing up to a computer is not something that you would get to do very often. So, there is a risk that precious photos and important information could be lost if something happens to your device and it has been a while since the last backup.

Wouldn't it be great if your backup happened daily, without you having to remember to do it? This is the **iCloud Backup** feature of iCloud.

You can still back up to iTunes

Even if you backup to iCloud, you can still choose to also do a backup to iTunes on your computer.

In fact, backing up to iTunes may be something you choose to do when you switch to a new iPhone or iPad. Instead of restoring from iCloud, you can restore from your iTunes backup – which can be faster than an iCloud restore.

Backing up iOS Devices to iCloud

Choosing to back up to iCloud

As mentioned earlier, go to **Settings -> [your-name] -> iCloud**.

Tap the **iCloud Backup** option, which is at the bottom of the second section.

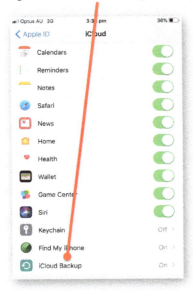

Turn **iCloud Backup** to on (green).

You can then choose **Back Up Now** if you would like to back up your device immediately.

The first backup may take quite a while, depending on how much data is stored on your iPad or iPhone, so make sure you stay connected to Wi-Fi and battery while this backup is completed.

If you stop the backup part-way through, it will need to start over again next time.

When does the iCloud Backup occur?

Your device will, from that point forward, perform a backup daily to iCloud whenever it detects that your iDevice satisfies all of the below conditions:

1. It is at least 24 hours since the last backup
2. i-Device is asleep
3. It is on Wi-Fi
4. It is being charged
5. There is enough space in your iCloud for the backup data

For me, this means that my backup generally occurs overnight while I sleep.

Backing up iOS Devices to iCloud

Viewing details of your iCloud Backups

This is managed from **Settings->[your-name]->iCloud,** by tapping the **Manage Storage** option that is under the coloured bar that shows your iCloud storage usage.

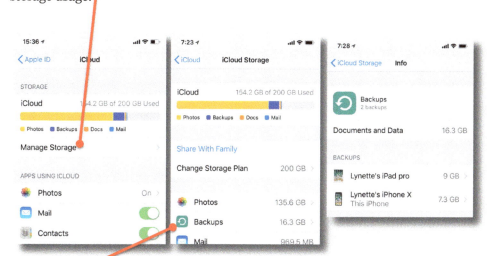

Tap the **Backups** option to see the details of your iCloud backups.

On the Mac, choose -> **System Preferences->iCloud** and click the **Manage Storage** option at bottom right.

Click the **Backups** option in the list that appears.

On both the iPad/iPhone and Mac, you will see the total amount of space being used by the **Documents and Data** in your iCloud Backup area, along with the list of devices for which iCloud is storing backups.

Backing up iOS Devices to iCloud

Later in this guide (from page 52), we will cover the topic of managing the iCloud data used by your iCloud backup, especially in cases where you run out of iCloud Storage. We will discuss at that point what to do about backups that you don't want to keep.

A full list of what does and doesn't back up to iCloud

Apple provides an excellent article that describes exactly what does and doesn't back up to iCloud.

It is included here for anyone who would like to read more about iCloud backups: **https://support.apple.com/kb/PH12519**

All about iCloud Drive

What is iCloud Drive

iCloud Drive is an area of iCloud that provides storage for:
- data associated with certain apps and
- those files and folders that you want to sync between your devices.

App Data in iCloud

iCloud Drive allows for the storage of App Data, so that this data can be synchronised between your iCloud and all your iCloud-enabled devices.

On the iPad and iPhone, turn on the **iCloud Drive** setting in **Settings->[your-name]-> iCloud**.

Then, any apps that are able to store their data in iCloud Drive are listed below that option.

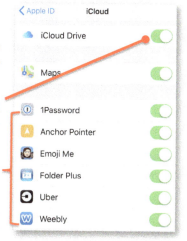

On the Mac, go to -> **System Preferences -> iCloud** and choose **Options** on the right of the iCloud Drive option. This will show the Mac apps that use your iCloud Drive.

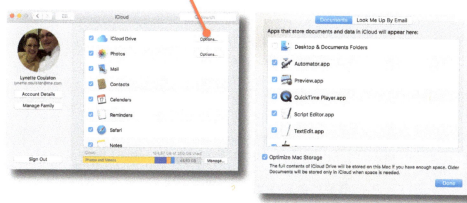

By syncing their data to iCloud, these apps will allow you to keep the app data synchronised between all your devices that use the apps.

This is especially useful for apps that provide both iPad and iPhone versions of the same app.

All about iCloud Drive

There are also some apps that have Mac versions (example are Apples Pages, Keynote and Numbers apps), so storing the app data in iCloud allows the mobile and computer devices to share the same information.

Turn to **on** any app whose data you wish to synchronise to your iCloud. Turn **off** any App you don't want to synchronise to iCloud and other devices.

Files and Folders in iCloud Drive

iCloud Drive also provides the ability to store any files you wish to synchronise between your devices.

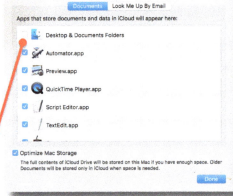

This provides a way of keeping your important files safely stored in iCloud, and readily available and retrievable should anything go wrong with any devices.

On your Mac, you can now choose to store your **Desktop** and **Documents** folders in your iCloud, which means the entire content of these folders is accessible from all your Apple devices – and even from any Web Browser!

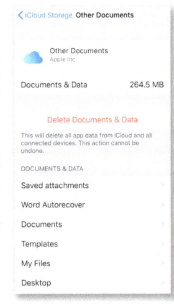

Ticking the top option in your Mac's iCloud Drive preferences (shown above right – see previous page for how to get to this screen) will move your **Desktop and Documents** folders (and their contents) to iCloud Drive

From either your Mac or your iOS devices, you can also (or instead) set up an alternative folder structure within your iCloud Drive to store and manage some or all of your files.

(This is the approach I prefer to take, instead of storing all of my Desktop and Documents in iCloud.)

All about iCloud Drive

Accessing iCloud Drive's folders and files on Mac

On the Mac, management of the files and folders in iCloud Drive is achieved from the **Finder** app, from the **iCloud Drive** entry in your Finder sidebar.

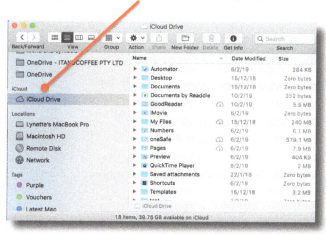

Accessing iCloud Drive's folders and files on iOS

A file management feature has been long awaited on the iPad and iPhone – and is now delivered by the **Files** app, which arrived with iOS 11.

We will talk about the **Files** app on page 65, but it is good to know that you can also see the files and folders that are stored in your iCloud Drive from the **Manage Storage** option of **Settings -> [your-name]->iCloud** on the iPad and iPhone.

Tap on the **iCloud Drive** app in the list of apps that is shown in the **Manage Storage** option

This will show a screen with the heading of **Other Documents** (as shown on the previous page), the total amount of storage used by these files, and the list of folders and files that are stored in iCloud Drive.

We'll look shortly (from page 52) at how to manage the file and folder storage aspect of iCloud Drive.

All about iCloud Drive

Preventing iCloud Drive from using Mobile Data

On an iPhone and cellular-enabled iPad, it is important to note that you can choose whether to allow your iCloud Drive to transfer/sync data only over Wi-Fi, or over both Wi-Fi and the mobile (cellular/3G/4G) network.

This is only applicable on your iPhone and cellular-enabled iPad.

To turn off the use of your mobile data for this purpose, go into **Settings -> Mobile** (sometimes this setting is Mobile Data, Cellular and Cellular Data).

Turn off the **iCloud Drive** option towards the bottom of the page to disable the use of cellular data for this purpose.

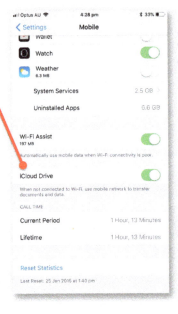

If this option is left switched on, your iCloud Drive can be updated any time your device has either a Wi-Fi signal or cellular signal.

Given that files in iCloud Drive can be very big, this could cause you to very quickly exceed you monthly mobile data allowance.

For most people, my recommendation is to turn this setting to Off.

"My iCloud is Full – what can I do?"

This is a question we get at iTandCoffee every week. What do you do when your iCloud is full?

You have two options when you get this message:

1. Free up some iCloud storage or
2. Purchase a plan that gives you additional storage

In this section we will cover how to check what is using all your iCloud, and how to free up storage that does not need to be used.

Options for reducing iCloud storage.

There are several things to consider when it comes to managing your iCloud storage.

- Do you have (and do you want) your Photos library stored in iCloud?
- Do you have excess device backups in iCloud that can be removed?
- Are there apps that don't need to be backed up to iCloud?
- Do you have apps unnecessarily using iCloud to store and sync data (e.g. games that the kids have installed on your device)?
- Are there files and folders stored in iCloud that don't need to be there?

As mentioned earlier, to look at what is using up all your iCloud storage on your iPad and iPhone, visit **Settings -> [your-name] -> iCloud -> Manage Storage**

On your Mac, go to -> **System Preferences** -> **iCloud**, and choose **Manage** at bottom right.

"My iCloud is Full – what can I do?"

Do you store your Photos library in iCloud?

We will talk about Photos in iCloud at length later in this guide (from page 88), but for now let's just look at the Photos setting in iCloud and how you work out whether your photos library is gobbling up all (or a large chunk) of your iCloud storage.

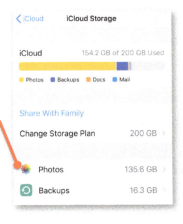

The **Photos** option in iCloud Storage shows the total amount of iCloud storage used by **iCloud Photos**.

If you see any storage value for Photos (in the example on the right, my Photos are using 135.6 GB of iCloud Storage!), it means that:

- you are currently using **iCloud Photos** on one or more of your devices or
- you have turned on **iCloud Photos** at some time – perhaps on another device - and then turned it off again

Once **iCloud Photos** is enabled, it starts uploading photos to iCloud – so that, even if you turn it off, there may still be photos taking up space in your iCloud.

If you are no longer using **iCloud Photos** and find that there are still photos stored in iCloud that have not been removed:

- On the iPad/iPhone, tap the **Photos** option in **Manage Storage**
- On the Mac, click the **Photos** option in **Manage**

You will have the option to **Disable & Delete** all the photos that are stored in iCloud Photos.

But Beware!

Just be aware that, if you still have iCloud Photos enabled on any devices, you will be removing those photos from those devices as well as from iCloud when you choose to **Disable & Delete**.

"My iCloud is Full – what can I do?"

So, before you choose **Disable & Delete**, make sure that iCloud Photos has been turned off on ALL devices and that you REALLY want to delete the photos from iCloud.

More detail on iCloud Photos is provided from page 90.

Do you have excess iOS backups in iCloud?

Over time, your iCloud can get clogged up with backups from devices that you no longer use – or with backups from devices that are not even yours!

As we have described earlier, the **Manage Storage** screen in your iCloud Settings / System Preferences, the **Backups** option shows how much of your iCloud storage is being used by backups.

Tap this **Backups** option to view further details of these backups.

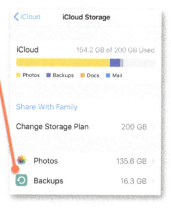

On the Mac, you will simply see a list of backups and be able to select one and choose to delete it.

On the iPad and iPhone, the top section of the Info screen shows a summary of the backups in your iCloud – how many you have, and their total storage.

Below that is a list of device backups that are stored in your iCloud.

Your current device's backup will have This iPhone (or This iPad) underneath.

If you see a backup for any device that is no longer in use, belongs to someone else, or is not required, tap on that item in the list.

You will see the details of that backup – the device name, when it was last backed up, and the size.

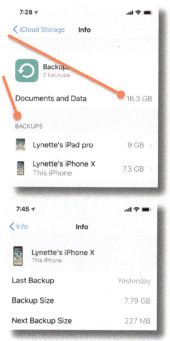

"My iCloud is Full – what can I do?"

If the backup was recent and does not seem to belong to one of your own devices, you may have a case of **iCloud Confusion** – i.e. someone else is also using your iCloud.

It is recommended that you sort this out before you delete their backup. (See the last section in this guide – from page 103.)

If the backup is not required, choose **Delete Backup**.

This could free up a huge chunk of iCloud space immediately!

Are there iOS apps that don't need to back up?

On your iPad or iPhone, touch on the backup for the **current device** (i.e. the backup that has This iPhone or This iPad beneath it, as described above).

You will then see the details of the next backup's size for the device, when the latest backup occurred, and how much space is needed in your iCloud for the next backup.

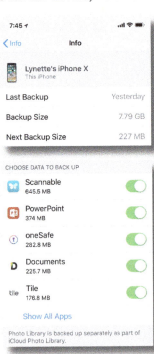

Below that is the list of all the apps whose data is being backed up to your iCloud (for the device that you selected).

To see the full list of apps that are on your device (and, potentially being backed up), tap on **Show All Apps**.

For each app, you can see the amount of storage that is currently being used by the backup of that app's data.

If you want to avoid backing up apps that don't need to be backed up, turn the applicable switch/es to 'off' (not green) for those apps.

This will remove the backup of that app from iCloud and free up the amount of storage that was listed for that app.

"My iCloud is Full – what can I do?"

This will not delete the app's data from your device – it will simply prevent the app from being backed up in future.

If anything happens to your device, you will not be able to restore that app's data to its previous state when you restore from your iCloud backup.

Are unnecessary apps syncing data using iCloud?

As mentioned earlier, certain apps will store their data in iCloud – to allow syncing with other devices.

On iPad and iPhone, these apps are listed under the **iCloud Drive** setting in **Settings -> [your-name] -> iCloud**. You will only see these listed apps if **iCloud Drive** is turned on.

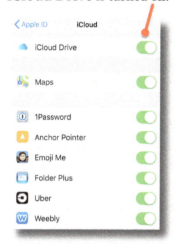

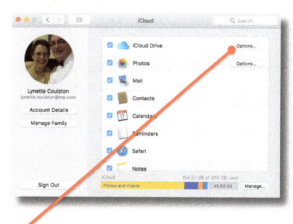

On Mac, view the apps that are using iCloud in -> **System Preferences -> iCloud,** by selecting the **Options** button on the right of the **iCloud Drive** option – again, this will only be visible if **iCloud Drive** is turned on.

If you don't need certain apps to store their data in iCloud – for example, any games the kids might have added to your device(!) – simply turn off that app in the list.

"My iCloud is Full – what can I do?"

The data for the app will then only be stored locally, on the current device.

Alternatively, just turn off **iCloud Drive** entirely if you don't want any apps on your device to be storing their data in iCloud.

This will also prevent you from using iCloud Drive to store and sync files and folders using your iCloud.

What apps are using the most iCloud storage?

On the iPad and iPhone, the **Manage Storage** option shows how much storage each app uses in your iCloud Drive.

The apps using your iCloud Drive are listed below the **Change Storage Plan** option and are ordered from largest storage user to smallest

All apps that use iCloud Drive are shown, including apps that are <u>not on the current device</u>.

On the Mac, you will see the list of iCloud-using apps by tapping **Manage** at the bottom right of the -> **System Preferences - > iCloud** screen.

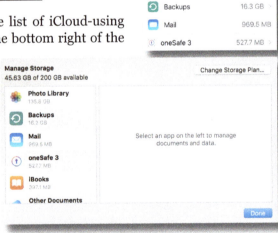

Apps listed in iCloud Drive could include those that you have previously deleted from your device/s, so you may no longer require their data.

Some may have been used on an older device and are no longer relevant.

They could be even apps that snuck their data into your iCloud when another person's device was also using your iCloud.

"My iCloud is Full – what can I do?"

Deleting App Data from iCloud

On the iPad/iPhone, if you decide that you don't need a particular app's data stored in iCloud, this data can be deleted by tapping on the app in the list shown above and choosing **Delete Documents & Data**.

For certain apps you will also see a list of items stored by that app, and be able to delete individual items instead of deleting ALL documents and data for the app.

For the Pages app shown in the example here, I can delete individual documents by swiping from right to left on the item in the list and choosing **Delete**.

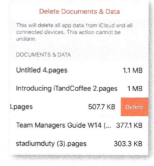

Just remember that, if you still have the app turned on in **Settings -> [your-name] -> iCloud**, any data you delete in **Manage Storage** will be gone from that App on all devices; and that data may be added back to iCloud as you continue to use the app.

On the **Mac**, the content of your **iCloud Drive** can be managed from your **Finder**, by visiting the **iCloud Drive** folder.

From here you can delete individual items associated with an App – or delete all data for the applicable app by deleting the app's folder. If you delete a folder, you will get a warning that the data will be deleted from ALL devices if you proceed.

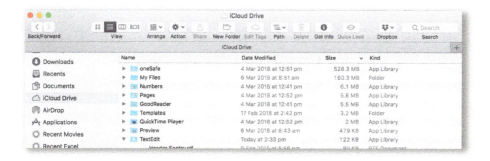

"My iCloud is Full – what can I do?"

Are files and folders using up space?

If you store files/folders in your iCloud Drive (Desktop and Documents folders, or other folder/s you created in iCloud Drive), it is possible to view and manage their storage from the **Manage Storage** option on your iPad and iPhone.

As mentioned earlier, the **iCloud Drive** option shows the files and folders stored in iCloud and how much storage they use.

Tap this option to view what is stored there.

If you see any folder or file that is no longer required, you can swipe from right to left to delete it.

To see more detail of any folder that is listed, tap on it to view a similar screen to that shown to that on the right allowing you to delete all the contents of the folder OR just individual items.

If you don't want any of these files and folders, you can delete the lot by selecting **Delete Documents & Data**

(As already mentioned, on the Mac, you can view and manage your iCloud Drive files from Finder.)

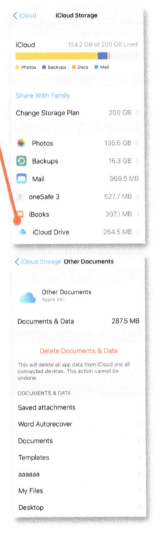

Moving Desktop & Documents out of iCloud

Are your Mac's Desktop & Documents folders stored in iCloud?

You can easily see from your Finder app on the Mac if your **Desktop** and **Documents** folders have been moved into iCloud. [2]

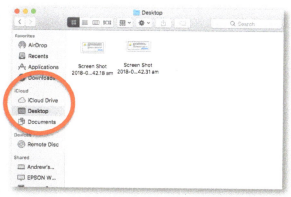

Desktop and **Documents** are folders that normally appear in the **Favourites** list of the Finder Sidebar, which is the top section of the sidebar.

However, if these folders have been moved to iCloud, you will instead see them under a separate **iCloud** section in the sidebar

If your **Documents** and **Desktop** appear in this section, every file and folder that you store in these folders will be taking up space in your iCloud.

If you decide that you do not want these folders to be taking up this space in iCloud– and that you don't require that the Desktop and Documents folders sync to your other devices – there are several steps to take to move these folders out of iCloud and revert to using just local Mac storage.

Your first step is to go to your **System Preferences** and turn off storage of **Desktop & Documents Folders** in iCloud.

---

[2] We won't attempt to explain Mac's Finder app, and how to manage your files and folders, as part of this guide. Instead, refer to iTandCoffee's guide '**Introduction to the Mac – Files, Folders and Finder**' if you need a comprehensive guide on this topic. Visit **itandcoffee.com.au/guides** for more information.)

Moving Desktop & Documents out of iCloud

Visit ->**System Preferences->iCloud** and tap the **Options** button on the right of the **iCloud Drive** option. Untick the **Desktop & Documents Folders** option

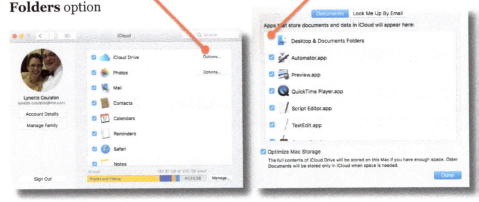

A warning message will appear – choose **Turn Off** to proceed.

Empty **Desktop** and **Documents** folders will appear in the **Favourites** sidebar of **Finder**. The **iCloud** section will only show **iCloud Drive** now.

The confusing thing is that your **Desktop** and **Documents** files will still be in iCloud Drive, in folders still called **Desktop** and **Documents**.

These are different folders to the **Desktop** and **Documents** in the **Favourites** section.

Further steps are required to put any files that were in the iCloud version of **Desktop** and **Documents** back into the local version of these folders shown in Favourites (where **local** means not stored just on the computer, not in iCloud).

To complete the removal of your Desktop and Documents contents from iCloud, you need to go to the iCloud Drive versions of these folders

Select the full contents of the Desktop (or Documents) folder that is still in iCloud Drive.

Moving Desktop & Documents out of iCloud

You can use Command-A to **select all** items in the folder. Drag the selected items across to the corresponding **Local** version of the Desktop or Documents folder in the **Favourites** section of the sidebar.

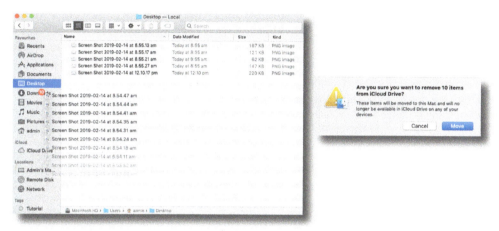

A warning will appear (see above right), advising that you will be removing the files from iCloud.

Choose **Move** to complete the removal of the selected files/folders from iCloud and return them to the local version of the Desktop or Documents folder.

Once the content of the **iCloud Drive** versions of **Desktop** and **Documents** have been moved back to the local version of that folder, you can delete the iCloud Drive versions of these folders.

(Note. You may find that these folders keep re-appearing. I have previously found that I need to log in to iCloud.com and visit the iCloud Drive option, then delete these folders from there. Only then do they stop re-appearing when I delete them from iCloud Drive in Finder.)

Getting additional iCloud storage

On your iPad and iPhone, visit **Settings -> [*your-name*] -> iCloud -> Manage Storage** (see below left).

On a Mac, visit -> **System Preferences -> iCloud** and choose the **Manage** option at bottom right (on the right of the storage usage bar – see above right).

Choose the option to **Change Storage Plan** (or it might say **Buy More Storage**).

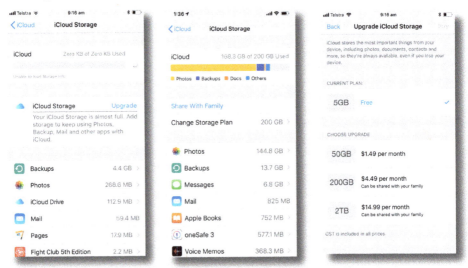

If you are close to running out of storage, you may see a message like that in the leftmost image above – in which case, choose **Upgrade**.

Currently, you can choose a 50GB plan, a 200GB plan and a 2TB plan.

Tap the option that you would like to choose and then tap **Buy** at the top right.

Getting additional iCloud storage

You will then need to approve the purchase of the monthly plan by entering your iCloud password.

The cost of your new storage plan will be charged monthly to your Apple account, to the credit card that is recorded against your iCloud's Apple ID.

If you have enabled something called **Family Sharing** (see page 85), you can choose to share the 200GB or 2TB plan with family members.

If you find that you have more storage than needed, you can **downgrade** your storage plan from this same option.

Managing your iCloud Drive Files on iOS

On a Mac, it is very easy to manage your **iCloud Drive** using the **Finder** app. This allows you to create your own folders, store files, delete files and folders, move content around, and more – all the standard **Finder** functionality.

The same applies on a Windows computer – the files in iCloud Drive can be managed from Windows File Explorer, from the iCloud Drive folder. This iCloud Drive folder is put in the Quick Access menu when you install iCloud for Windows. It is also available from the Start menu.

But how do you store and manage files on an iPad and iPhone?

Introducing the Files App

A new app arrived in iOS 11 in 2017, one that provides a File Management capability on the iPad and iPhone.

This app is called **Files**.

We will not seek to cover all of the functionality associated with the **Files** app here (which includes the ability to view all your Cloud services – such as Dropbox, OneDrive and Google Drive - from one place).

Rather, we will focus on how the **Files** app can provide an easy way of managing your **iCloud Drive** file storage to:

- Create folders in iCloud Drive – including sub-folders within folders
- Move files and folders between folders, to create a structure that allows you to easily find your saved information
- Delete folders and files that are no longer needed

Tap on the **Files** app to open it.

You will see there are two options along the bottom – **Recent** and **Browse**.

Managing your iCloud Drive Files on iOS

Tap **Browse** to browse your files and folders and to find your **iCloud Drive** folder.

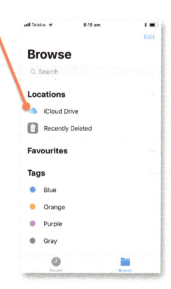 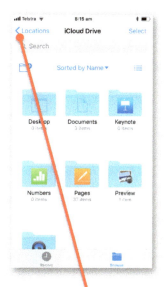

If you do not see **Browse** screen (as shown above left), < at top left until you do.

Tap on the **iCloud Drive** folder to see a list of folders and files (as shown in the image above right).

These folders can be viewed as icons (as shown in the image above right) or as a list. Tap the **list** symbol ≡ to switch to 'list' view – shown on the right.

If you are not seeing the **list** symbol ≡ towards the top right of the screen, drag downwards to reveal it.

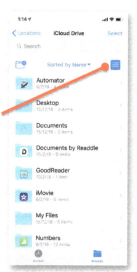

The folders you see in iCloud Drive depend on your own iCloud Drive contents and the apps that you have on the iOS device.

Some of the folders are for apps that store their data in your iCloud. You will generally want to leave these ones alone.

Managing your iCloud Drive Files on iOS

If you have a Mac, and you have chosen to store your **Desktop** and **Documents** folders in iCloud Drive (as described earlier), you will see these folders (and their contents) in the **iCloud Drive** folder on your iPad and iPhone.

Creating Folders & Sub-Folders in iCloud Drive

In your iCloud Drive folder, you can create your own folders and sub-folders for storing any files that you wish to save away - for example, from emails or messages, saved PDFs of web pages, Airdropped files, and more.

By saving them to iCloud Drive, you will also be saving them to your iCloud (so that they are safe if something happens to your device).

You will find the **add folder** option just below the search bar.

If you don't see this option (or the Search bar), drag down slightly on the middle of the screen to uncover this option – as well as options for sorting (sort by name, date, size or tag) and choosing your folder view (list or icon view).

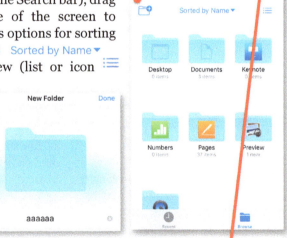

Tap the **add folder** symbol, then tap below the folder symbol in the box provided to enter the name for your new folder. Then choose **Done** at top right.

You can then tap on that new folder and follow the same steps to create a sub-folder within that new folder.

Moving Items between Folders in iCloud Drive

To move any files and folders into a different folder, tap Select at the top right.

Select each item that you wish to move by tapping it.

Managing your iCloud Drive Files on iOS

If you are in list view, a tick will appear on the left of each item you select. If you are in icon view, the tick will appear on the file/folder icon.

Choose the **move** symbol from the toolbar at the bottom.

Then, navigate your way to the folder to which you wish to move the selected items.

Note that the folder must already exist – you can't create a new folder as part of this move process.

Tap the folder, then choose **Move** at top right to complete the move. In the above example, I tapped the **aaaaaa** folder then **Move**.

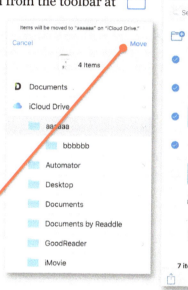
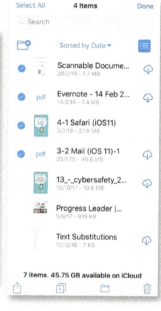

Delete files or folders in iCloud Drive

Follow the same steps described above for selecting the set of files/folders you wish to delete.

Then choose the trash can (at bottom right) to delete these files.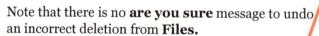

Note that there is no **are you sure** message to undo an incorrect deletion from **Files**.

Files that you delete will be moved to **Recently Deleted,** which can be found at the top level of the **Browse** screen.

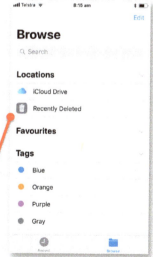

Managing your iCloud Drive Files on iOS

Recovering Deleted items in iCloud Drive

If you ever delete a file or folder from your iCloud Drive, then decide later that you would like to get it back, visit the **Recently Deleted** folder of the Files app.

From this folder, you can choose to restore any previously deleted items you find there (as long as you do so within about 30 days of their deletion).

To choose one or more files to recover (or to permanently delete these files), choose Select at top right, then tap the files/folders that you wish to select.

Then choose the Recover option at the bottom to restore the selected files/folders to their previous location.

Or choose the Delete option to permanently delete the selected files/folders.

It is important to note that you will not find this **Recently Deleted** folder in iCloud Drive on your Mac, so it is handy to know it is accessible from your iPad or iPhone if you do find that you are missing an important file that had been stored in your **iCloud Drive**.

Accessing your iCloud from Any Computer

Your iCloud accessible from any computer

From any computer, you can access your iCloud information from a web browser (for example, Chrome, Internet Explorer, Edge, Firefox, Safari).

There are lots of reasons why such access to your iCloud can be helpful – we'll touch on some of these reasons in this section.

Visit the website **www.icloud.com**.

Log in with your iCloud Apple ID and password. If required, enter the verification code that appears on one of your other Apple Devices – to confirm that you are the owner of the iCloud account. (We cover about this verification code and two-factor-authentication from page 73.)

You then have access to a range of iCloud data and apps.

Accessing your iCloud from Any Computer

View and manage Photos in iCloud

If iCloud Photos is enabled on any device, the photos from that and other devices will be shown in the Photos option. From this area of iCloud.com, you can create albums and folders and do a variety of other things to manage you Photos library.

Pages, Keynote, Numbers editing from a Web Browser

If you have turned on **iCloud Drive**, you will even have access to any view and edit any **Pages**, **Keynote** and **Number**s documents from the web browser (even if you are on a Windows computer).

Manage iCloud Drive content

If iCloud Drive is enabled on any of your devices, the files and folders that are stored in your **iCloud Drive** can be viewed and managed from the **iCloud Drive** app of iCloud.com.

Recover deleted iCloud Drive files

Files deleted from iCloud Drive will be temporarily saved to a **Recently Deleted** folder, which is accessible from the **iCloud Drive** app of iCloud.com.

The number of recently deleted items is shown at the bottom right of the **iCloud Drive** page. Click this to view these recently deleted items – and to recover them or permanently delete them.

Find a lost device

Visit iCloud.com to search for a lost Mac, iPad or iPhone using the **Find iPhone** app that is available there.

Manage Contacts

If you end up with lots of duplicated contacts, it can be easier to sort out these duplicates from iCloud.com, since you can select many items in the list of contacts and delete them in one hit.

Accessing your iCloud from Any Computer

You can also create groups of contacts from iCloud.com – something that is not available in the standard iOS **Contacts** app.

Recover Contacts, Calendar, Reminders, Bookmarks

Another important thing to know about iCloud.com is that it gives access to some options that are not available elsewhere.

In the **Settings** app of iCloud.com, you will see some options at the bottom, under the **Advanced** heading.

These options provide **Restore** capabilities for files, contacts, calendars, reminders and bookmarks that you may have inadvertently deleted, and now wish to retrieve.

Set up 'Out of Office' reply for iCloud mail

If you want an automatic reply to be sent for any email your iCloud mail account receives, choose the **Mail** app from iCloud.com, choose the **Settings** symbol at bottom left, and choose **Preferences**. Choose the **Vacation** option at the top.

Set up rules for your iCloud email

The Preferences option of the Mail app in iCloud.com also allows the set-up of Rules for your mail - to automatically organise, delete, flag/mark, or forward your mail as it arrives.

Ensuring the security of your iCloud

Use a Strong, Different Password

As for all online accounts, it is essential to ensure that your iCloud account has a strong password, and that this password is different to your other online account passwords.

Two-step verification

To help keep your Apple accounts safe, in recent years Apple has added improved security for these accounts.

At first, this security came in the form of **two-step verification** – where a text would be sent to your mobile phone when a sign in to iCloud was attempted, providing a verification code that had to be entered in addition to the iCloud email address and password.

Some Apple accounts will still be set up to use this two-step verification.

Two-Factor-Authentication

More recently, Apple updated this security to something called **two-factor authentication** – which means that you must provide a second form of authentication in addition to your password.

If you attempt to sign in to your Apple ID from a device that is not listed as an **approved** device for that Apple ID (or sign in from a web browser), you will get a message popping up on at least one of your approved device/s.

Even though the location shown on the message that you see may not actually be your current location, if you just tried to sign in to your Apple account, it is safe to choose **Allow** to get a 6-digit verification code.

Ensuring the security of your iCloud

Enter this verification code on the device that is being signed in. That device will then become an approved device for that Apple account.

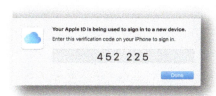

Setting up Two-Factor-Authentication

This two-factor-authentication is set up from
Settings -> [your-name] on your iPad and iPhone,
or from -> **System Preferences -> iCloud** on your Mac.

You may see a message at the top showing that you need to set up this security feature (see below). If you see this, select that option to set up the essential security feature.

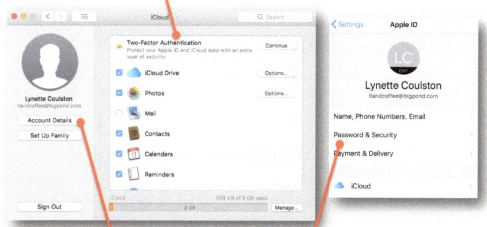

If no such message is showing, choose:

- **Account Details** option on the Mac
- The **Password and Security** option on the iPad / iPhone. Choose the **Account Details** option

You will be asked to answer two of your security questions to access this option.

Ensuring the security of your iCloud

Then, you will see the option to **Turn on Two-Factor Authentication**.

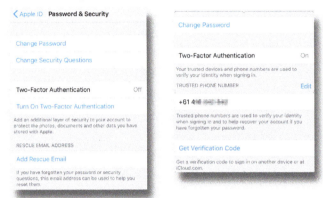

You will need to confirm the phone number that can be used as an alternative means of verification – a text will be sent to that mobile with a code to confirm the mobile number is valid.

Once two-factor authentication is set up, you will be able to come to this same screen to **Get Verification Code** for this Apple account – should you ever need one.

iCloud sign ins on older devices

A word of warning if you still have a Mac that is running OSX 10.10 or earlier, an iPad or iPhone that is running an older version of iOS, or perhaps an older Apple TV.

You will find that your password does not seem to work after you set up two-factor authentication on your newer device.

This is because your password alone is no longer adequate to sign in, but these older Apple operating systems are not 'aware' of the newer security measure.

The solution is to append the verification code to the end of the password (without a space between them). Visit **Settings -> [your-name] -> iCloud -> Password & Security** to **Get Verification Code** to use for this purpose.

You will only need to use this extended password once on that older device. After that, just your password (without verification code) should work.

If, at any point in future, you find your password does not seem to be working, try adding a verification code again to see if that works.

Managing your Apple ID from a Web Browser

There are two important Apple web pages to save away as bookmarks in your web browser.

They are **appleid.apple.com** and **iforgot.apple.com**.

appleid.apple.com

This web page allows you to manage and view all sorts of things to do with your Apple ID.

- Your name
- The email address you use as your Apple ID
- Your date of birth
- Country/region
- Password changes and two-factor authentication settings
- Trusted phone number
- Payment method
- Other contact email addresses
- Devices that are linked to the Apple ID

Managing your Apple ID from a Web Browser

Changing the email address of your iCloud account

Your iCloud's email address can be changed by visiting appleid.apple.com and choosing **Edit** in the Account section of the page.

This may be necessary in cases where you are no longer using the email address that you registered as your Apple ID.

While it is possible to change your account's email address, just be careful about how you go about doing this.

Before you visit appleid.apple.com to change the account's email address, it is essential that you make sure you **first sign out of iCloud** on each and every device that uses that Apple ID.

This sign-out is done from **Settings -> [your-name]** on the iPad & iPhone. The **Sign Out** option is at the very bottom of that screen.

On the Mac, sign out from **-> System Preferences-> iCloud**.

Determining which devices are signed in to your iCloud is quite easy these days – just visit the **Settings -> [your-name].** The list of devices that use the same Apple ID are shown at the bottom of that screen.

Once you have signed out of iCloud on all devices, go to **appleid.apple.com** and make the necessary change to the email address.

Managing your Apple ID from a Web Browser

You will be asked to verify your identity first by providing a two-factor authentication code provided on another of your Apple devices, or if you don't have two-factor authentication enabled, by answering two of your security questions.

Once you have made any change to your Apple account's email address, sign back in to iCloud on each device – using the new email address and the password that already applied (unless you changed this too).

If you fail to sign out of iCloud on all devices before you change your Apple ID, you can end up locked out of your iCloud account on those devices if you don't still have access to the old email address.

iforgot.apple.com

If you forget your Apple ID's password, resetting the password for your Apple ID can also be done from your web browser, by visiting website **iforgot.apple.com**.

Enter the Apple ID that requires the password reset.

Refer to the next section for further description of how to reset your Apple account's password.

When you forget your Apple Password

Your Apple ID's password is a password that you will tend to enter more frequently than many other passwords, so it is important to try to remember it.

However, as we see at iTandCoffee week in and week out, it is very easy to forget one's Apple ID – especially if you haven't downloaded any apps for quite a while or if you tend to rely on Touch ID or Face ID for approving purchases.

If you need to change your Apple account's password, it doesn't have to be a stressful exercise any more – especially if you have set up two-factor authentication.

Change your Apple account's password using your iOS device's Passcode

If you are on the latest iOS version on your iPad or iPhone, you can change your Apple ID's password from the **Settings** app – without having to know your current password.

Tap on your name at the top of Settings, and then the **Password & Security** option. Tap **Change Password**

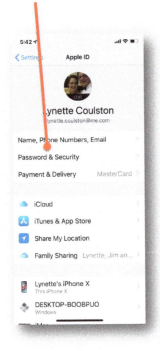
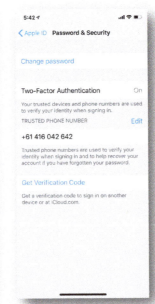

When you forget your Apple Password

At the top of that screen is the **Change password** option (see previous page). Tap this, then enter your iPhone's or iPad's passcode.

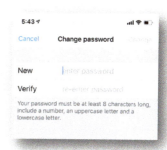

You will then be able to enter (and re-enter) a new password for your Apple ID.

What are the rules for Apple passwords?

This new password must be at least 8 characters, must include at least one uppercase, lowercase and a number. It usually can't just be a word and number or a name and number, so try substituting numbers or symbols for letters.

Choose **Change** at top right once you have done this.

Change your Apple ID's password from your Mac

On a Mac, visit -> **System Preferences** -> **iCloud**, and select **Account Details**. Click the **Security** option along the top, and you will see the **Change Password** option.

Enter your Mac's user account password (the one you use to unlock your Mac) to gain access to the **Change Password** screen, from which you can enter the new password, then choose the **Change** option.

80

When you forget your Apple Password

If you don't have these password reset options

You may not have the option to reset a forgotten Apple password from the **Password & Security** option, as it may ask you for the current Apple password to access the option. This is no help if you don't know that password!

This will occur if the device you are using is not a trusted device for the Apple ID – usually because you have not set up two-factor-authentication.

On the Mac, simply choose the Forgot Password? option on the right of the password text box and choose to **Reset by Email** or **Answer Security Questions**.

On the iPad or iPhone, go to the **Settings** app, tap your name at the top, choose the **iTunes and App Store** option and tap the blue Apple ID at the top.

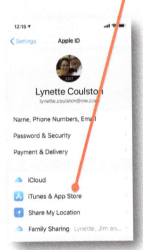
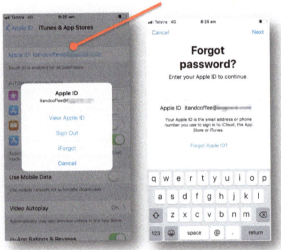

You will see a screen that allows you to choose the iForgot option to change your password.

Follow the prompts to choose to **Reset by email** or **Answer security questions**.

If you have access to the email identified by the Apple ID, **Reset by email** is generally the easier option for resetting.

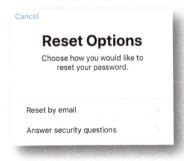

When you forget your Apple Password

If you must answer the security questions, you need to ensure that your answers are exactly correct – with correct upper or lower-case letters, and with any spaces, etc., that you used.

Resetting your password using iforgot.apple.com

As mentioned earlier, resetting the password for your Apple ID can also be done from any web browser, by visiting **iforgot.apple.com**.

Enter the Apple ID that requires a password reset.

Once again, the way in which you reset the password depends on whether you have set up two-factor authentication.

As described earlier, if you don't have two-factor authentication, iforgot.apple.com will allow you to choose to receive a password reset link in an email, or whether to answer two of your security questions.

If you are using two-factor authentication for your Apple account, you will be asked to enter the mobile phone number associated with your Apple ID.

You will then be presented with a screen showing instructions for resetting your password using one of your Apple ID's **Trusted Devices**. A notification will appear on each trusted device. Here is the notification on my Mac – in which case I choose **Show** and then set my new password.

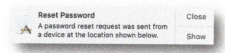

When you forget your Apple Password

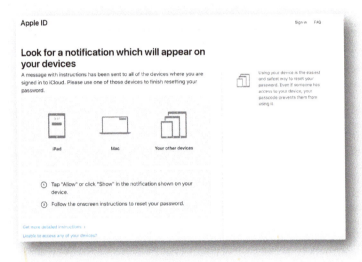

If you don't have access to any of the **Trusted Devices**, choose the Unable to access any of your devices? option at the bottom to see the screen below.

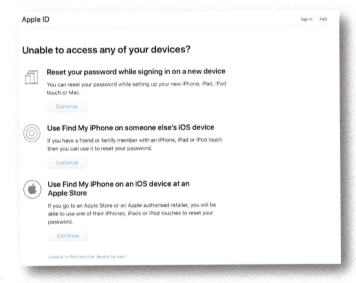

You will see that you can use the **Find my iPhone** app on someone else's iOS device to perform the password reset. For this option to work, you will need access to the mobile phone that is connected to your Apple ID – so that an SMS security code can be sent to that device.

When you forget your Apple Password

If you don't have access to that phone, your password reset will be more difficult and will take at least several days. This is so that Apple can be absolutely sure that your account and data is not being compromised or stolen.

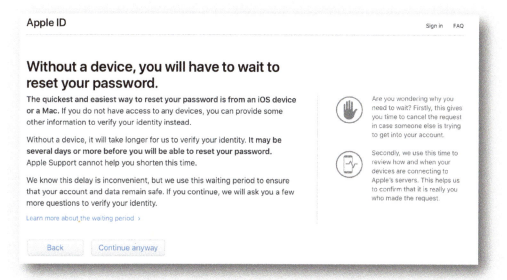

We won't go into this area further here. Hopefully your password reset won't require that you utilize this option.

Family Sharing

Introducing Family Sharing

In 2014, Apple introduced the **Family Sharing** feature. This feature now allows:

- families to share each other's purchases made using iTunes
- parents to approve (or not) purchases made by children
- family members to optionally share their location with each other
- family members to share Family events in the Calendar
- iCloud storage to be shared (i.e. share the cost, but still keep iCloud data separate)
- Photos to be shared between family members
- An Apple Music subscription to be shared by family members
- Parents to manage and monitor their child's **Screen Time**

Setting up Family Sharing

One person in the family sets themselves up as the 'organiser' of the family, and then invites other members of the family to join the iCloud Family.

To set up your Family, visit **Settings->[your-name]->Set up Family Sharing** on the iPad or iPhone.

On the Mac, visit -> **System Preferences -> iCloud** and select **Set Up Family**.

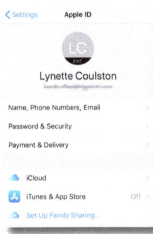

When you choose to **Get Started**, you will see several **Family Sharing** options are available (as shown in the far right images).

Simply choose what you would like to share, and then follow

Family Sharing

the prompts to invite others to share your purchase, music and/or iCloud storage.

To share Purchases, Apple Music or Storage, there must be a credit card registered with your Apple account, and this is the card that will be debited for any family member purchases/payments.

If you choose to share your Purchases, Family members can be invited by sending an invitation to them via iMessage (**Invite via iMessage**).

The recipient accepts the invitation on their own device by signing into their iCloud account.

Alternatively, you can **Invite in Person**, getting that person to sign in to their iCloud account on your device.

Both of these options assume the family member has an Apple ID. If this is not the case, a child who is 13 or over can create their own Apple ID. Refer earlier in this guide (page 32) for details on how to do this.

For a child who is under 13, choose the **Create a Child Account** option and follow the prompts to create that child's account. In particular, turn on the **Ask to Buy** setting so that you can approve any App requests your child makes – even when you are not with them!

On the family member devices, make sure each person signs in to **iCloud** and **iTunes & App Store** with their own Apple ID.

If they are currently signed in with a shared Apple ID, refer to the last section in this guide for details of how to remedy this (from page 103).

Family Sharing

Sharing iCloud Storage with the Family

If you upgrade your iCloud Storage to the 200GB or 2TB plan, this iCloud Storage can be shared with members of your family – so that they don't have to pay a separate monthly subscription for their iCloud storage.

Sharing this storage does not mean that your iClouds are shared or merged. It simply means that you share the storage allocation.

Individual family members can continue to pay for their own storage if desired – they don't have to share your storage allowance.

Sharing your Location with your Family

The **Location Sharing** option in Family Sharing allows family members to share their location with other family members, through the **Find my Friends** or **Find my iPhone** apps.

Adjusting your Family Sharing settings

Once Family Sharing has been set up, the settings and members can be viewed and updated from **Settings -> [your-name] -> Family Sharing** on the iPad and iPhone, from -> **System Preferences -> iCloud -> Manage Family** on the Mac.

Photos in iCloud

There are three aspects of iCloud that relate to your photos and videos. These are:

- iCloud Photos
- My Photo Stream
- Shared Albums

For any of these options to be available for the Photos app, your iPad, iPhone, Mac or Windows computer must be signed in to your iCloud account.

To see your settings for Photos in iCloud on iOS and Mac, go to:

on the iPad & iPhone, **Settings->[your-name]-> iCloud->Photos**

on the Mac, **-> System Preferences-> iCloud** and tap the **Options** button on the right of the **Photos** option.

The same options appear on all devices – below shows a couple of examples of what you might see when you visit the **iCloud Photos** option.

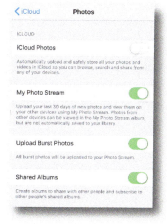 

Photos in iCloud

Here is a summary of what each of the three iCloud photos features offers. We will then cover each of these areas in further detail in the next few sections of the guide.

iCloud Photos Stores all your photos in iCloud and allows each of your devices to view and manage this same set of photos and Albums.

Extra iCloud storage may be needed to store large libraries, and devices that can't fit the entire library will need to **optimise** the storage of the photos/videos and may need internet access when viewing photos. *(Note. Windows computers can also use iCloud Photos, although syncing is not automatic.)*

My Photo Stream Allows streaming of photos (not videos) between your iCloud-enabled devices, including Windows computers, whenever those devices are connected to Wi-Fi.

My Photo Stream photos are only held in iCloud for 30 days, and only the last 1000 Photo Stream photos are stored on your Apple mobile devices.

My Photo Stream DOES NOT offer permanent storage of your photos in iCloud.

If you don't see the My Photo Stream option in your Preferences, it is because this feature is no longer available for newer iCloud accounts (as Apple is wanting people to use iCloud Photos instead).

Shared Albums Allows creation of special Shared Albums in iCloud that can be then shared with other people.

The great news is that Shared Albums do not add to your iCloud storage usage. A Shared Album can have up to 5000 items in it.

iCloud Photos

iCloud Photos (previously called iCloud Photo Library) was introduced in April 2015. It provides centralised storage of all your photos in iCloud and allows the viewing and updating of the photos library in iCloud from any devices connected to that iCloud account.

Your iCloud Photos Options

Depending on the amount of storage on your device, you can choose in your **Photos** Settings/Preferences whether you wish to:

- **Download and Keep Originals** - Store all your photos and videos on your device (which you will only be able to choose if you have sufficient storage for your entire photos library) or
- **Optimise iPhone Storage** - Reduce the storage used by your Photos library by optimizing it (which means viewing the full version of many photos and videos will require internet access

The great benefits of iCloud Photos

There are many great reasons for using iCloud Photos:

- Photos and videos are synchronised between all devices that are connected to the iCloud Photos. This means you have your photos and videos at your fingertips whenever you need them
- Albums are synchronised - meaning that albums can be created on an iPhone, iPad and Mac, and be visible then on all other device
- Folders you create in your Mac's Photos app are synchronized to your iOS devices
- The **Favourites** album synchronises
- The **People** albums synchronise*
- Photos deleted on one device are also deleted on other devices
- Photo edits are synchronized across devices
- If your iPhone or iPad is lost – in fact, if all your devices are lost - your photos are safely stored and readily available in iCloud
- You can view your photos from a web browser, by visiting iCloud.com

* Assumes you have the latest iOS and MacOS operating systems.

iCloud Photos

For many people, this offers a great solution to storage of their photos and videos, allowing the Photos apps on iOS and MacOS to seamlessly manage your library of photos and videos. I do use this service on all my Apple devices.

The disadvantages of iCloud Photos

The problems can start when your Photos library is a large one.

iCloud Photos offers only an 'all or nothing' solution to storage of your photos on each device.

This means that, if iCloud Photos is turned on, the device will show EVERY photo and video that is in the library. You don't get to choose to selectively sync only certain albums to your Apple mobile devices and Mac.

Inability to access photos without internet

If your library is big, it may not fit on your mobile device/s. It may not even fit on your Mac if that device has only 128GB or 256GB of storage.

In this case, your device will store 'cut down' versions of some or all of your photos and videos – which means photos may be blurry and only able to be viewed properly once they are downloaded from your iCloud.

Videos may take a while to download and play, again using up internet download data (perhaps your mobile data).

This is referred to as **Optimised** storage of your Photos and Videos, where not all photos and videos in your Photos library are stored on your device. The thumbnail will show, but the photo itself may need to be downloaded from your iCloud.

You need internet access to view the **Optimised** photos and videos and usually have to endure a delay before you can see full resolution versions of your photos and videos.

Unexpected Mobile Data Use

This can result in unexpected mobile data usage, and great frustration at the delay in seeing a clear image, or at not being able to view photos and videos when there is no internet.

Added costs of iCloud Photos

I have chosen with my more recent iPhones to purchase larger capacity iPhones (i.e. 256GB) so that I can 'download and keep' my entire 160GB Photos library.

iCloud Photos

This, of course, means I paid a higher price for my device. Added to all this is the cost of storing all my photos and videos in iCloud, as I need to pay for the 200GB storage plan (at $4.49 per month).

Once you exceed your 5GB free storage limit for iCloud (which most people do if they use iCloud Backup and/or iCloud Photos), you have to start paying for your iCloud storage.

Photos on the Mac says there are no photos to import

We regularly see clients with this problem after they have (often accidentally) turned on iCloud Photos.

If you turn on iCloud Photos on a mobile device that has a small amount of storage (e.g. an iPad or iPhone with 16GB or 32GBof storage), you can find that you are no longer able to just plug your iPad/iPhone into your Mac and import new photos into the Photos App.

You may be told that there are no photos on your i-Device.

This is because your photos have been uploaded to iCloud, and only optimised versions of the photos have been left on the iPhone/iPad. These optimised versions cannot be imported to the Mac.

(The same applies if you try to import the photos to your Windows computer.)

You are left wondering where your Photos have gone, and how to get them onto your computer if you don't want to use iCloud Photos.

Should you use iCloud Photos?

iTandCoffee's recommendation is that you don't set up iCloud Photos unless you are fully aware of the implications and have the storage space to store your whole library on your device.

If iCloud Photos has been accidentally enabled, it can be tricky to undo. And you can find some unexpected consequences of turning this feature on or off.

iCloud Photos

Turning off iCloud Photos

You can turn off iCloud Photos by un-selecting the iCloud Photos option from:

- *on the iPad & iPhone,* **Settings->[your-name]-> iCloud->Photos**

- *on the Mac,* **->System Preferences-> iCloud** and tap the **Options** button on the right of the **Photos** option

If you had sufficient space for your Photos library on your device and you have selected to **Download and Keep Original**, turning off iCloud Photos should leave all photos and videos on your device.

If your device has the **Optimise Storage** option selected, some or all of the photos on your device could be low resolutions versions.

If there are any such photos on your device, turning off iCloud Photos (by turning off the iCloud Photos option in your settings/preferences) will require that you agree to remove these low-resolution photos/videos from your device.

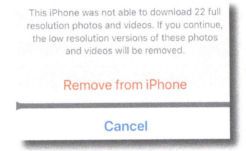

These items will still be available in your iCloud. But if you don't want to connect to iCloud Photos on any of your devices, how do you get your photos out of iCloud and onto your Mac, Windows computer, or elsewhere?

We cover this in the next section.

Getting your Photos out of iCloud Photos

If you have photos in iCloud Photos that you need to get out of iCloud, this is easy enough if you don't have too many. However, if you have a lot of photos to download from iCloud Photos, it can be a little trickier.

See your iCloud Photos in icloud.com

You can visit iCloud.com from your web browser and access the **Photos** app from this web page.

Choose the **Photos** or **Moments** options at the top to see all the photos that are stored in your iCloud Photos. You can also choose to hide or show the sidebar, which allows your photos to be viewed by media type, albums and more. Look for the Sidebar symbol at top left of the screen.

Download a selection of photos from iCloud.com

A set of several photos can be selected by holding the Command key on the Mac (or the Control key on Windows) as you click the required photos.

A consecutive set of photos can be selected by clicking on the first photo, then holding the Shift key as you click the last.

Or, from the Moments view, select all images for a day (or multiple days) by clicking the Select that appears top right of the relevant Moment/s.

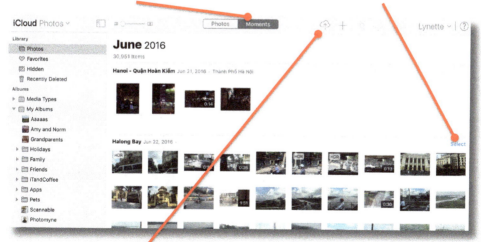

Then choose the download symbol at the top   to download the selected photos.

Getting your Photos out of iCloud Photos

You are limited to downloading 1000 items at a time – which can make the download process very tedious if, like me, you have large number of photos in iCloud.

Before you choose the **Download** option for the photos you have selected, there is something to consider.

Download originals or edited versions

You have a choice to either download the **Unmodified Original** or the versions of the photos that include any edits.

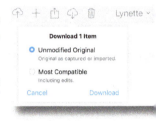

These options can be found by hovering your mouse over the 'download' symbol to expose a 'down-arrow' at bottom right of the symbol.

Click this down-arrow to expose the additional download options. Make your selection, then choose Download.

Where do the downloaded photos go?

Downloaded photos will go to your default **Downloads** location (usually your **Downloads** folder), as defined by your web browser's preferences.

On Windows, the downloaded file will be **iCloud Photos.zip** – which is a compressed file containing a folder with all your selected photos.

Open that .zip file to see this folder - called **iCloud Photos**. Simply move this folder and/or its contents to Pictures (or wherever you wish to put these photos).

On Mac, the download process creates either a folder or a .zip file in **Downloads**. Whether it creates a folder or .zip file depends on the total download size. A .zip file will be used if you download lots of photos/videos at once.

If a .zip file is downloaded, double-click the .zip file in Downloads when the download finishes – this will create a new **iCloud Photos** folder in Downloads, containing your downloaded photos & videos. Once that folder has been created, you can delete the separate .zip file.

If you have already done a previous download of photos to your from iCloud.com (and, as a result, the **iCloud Photos** zip or folder already exists in Downloads),

Getting your Photos out of iCloud Photos

the new folder or .zip name will have a sequential number appended – for example **iCloud Photos-2** on Mac and **iCloud Photos (2)** on Windows.

If you choose to download a large number of photos

If you choose to download a large number of photos – and especially if you download videos - be aware that this download may take some time (depending on your internet connection's download speed).

Any interruption to your internet connection during the download will stop the download in its tracks, and you will have to start all over again.

Of course, downloading a large Photos library in batches of 1000 items (and waiting for each batch to download) is not really a great solution if you have thousands or tens of thousands of photos to download from iCloud.

So, what other options do you have?

Temporarily turn on iCloud Photos on a Mac

You could turn on iCloud Photos on a computer that has sufficient storage capacity for this library. This could be done as a temporary or permanent solution.

For a Mac, this would download the complete iCloud-based library to your device, as long as you ensure that the **Download and Keep Originals** option is selected. This could take significant time, depending on the size of the library and your internet connection's download speed.

Unlike with downloading your photos 1000 at a time from iCloud.com, the downloading performed in this way will be able to 'pick up from where it left off' each time you disconnect from, then reconnect to the internet.

When the download completes, if you don't want to keep syncing with iCloud Photos, turn off iCloud Photos again in your Photos app's Preferences.

You can then delete the library from your iCloud using the methods described earlier for cleaning up iCloud storage.

Getting your Photos out of iCloud Photos

Before you turn on iCloud Photos on a Mac ...

If you choose to temporarily turn on iCloud Photos on your Mac, it may not be a good idea to do this from your existing Photos Library on the Mac, as this will result in your existing Photos library being merged with that in iCloud.

If your existing Photos library on the Mac is large, this process may take days and days before you see your downloaded iCloud photos, and may blow your iCloud data limit.

If this is not your intent, it is best to instead create a new, temporary, Photos Library and download the iCloud Photos to this library.

Create a temporary Photos library on Mac

This is done by holding down the **Option** key while you click the **Photos** app in the dock, giving you the **Choose Library** window, with the option to **Create New ...** (at the bottom).

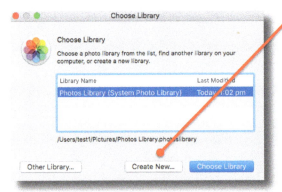

Choose the **Create New** option and create a new Photos library, which can be located on your Mac, or could be stored on an external device (e.g. a USB stick or external hard drive).

Once you choose the location and name for the temporary library, choose OK to open the Photos app for this new library.

You will then need to make this library the **System Photo Library**, so that it can sync with your iCloud Photos. (This will then need to be changed back to your *real* Photos library when you are done with downloading from iCloud.)

Go to **Photos->Preferences** and choose the **General** option along the top.

Getting your Photos out of iCloud Photos

Select the **Use as System Photo Library** option.

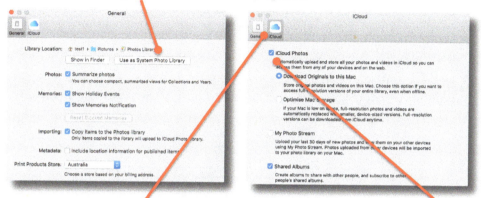

Then, select the **iCloud** option at the top of Photos Preferences and tick **iCloud Photos** to turn it on.

Turn off **My Photo Stream** and **Shared Albums**.

Then you will need to wait for all the photos to be downloaded from iCloud to this temporary Photos library. This could take days – depending on the speed of your internet downloads and how many photos need to be downloaded from iCloud.

Once you have all the photos downloaded to this temporary Photos library, turn off iCloud Photos (in Photos Preferences) for this temporary library.

Re-instate the *real* Photos library

When the downloads complete, you'll need to make your *real* Photos library the **System Photo Library** again.

Do this by using the **Option** key again while clicking the **Photos** app in the Dock and choosing your 'real' library from the list shown.

Go to **Photos->Preferences->General** and click **Use as System Photo Library** to again make that library your main Photos library.

Merging downloaded photos with real library

If you want to merge that temporary Photos library with your real library, this is a little tricky as well, as there is no Apple-provided tool to merge photos libraries.

Getting your Photos out of iCloud Photos

You have the option to export some or all photos from the temporary library and then import them to your *real* Photos library.

(Refer to iTandCoffee's '**Photos on the Mac**' guide for more information about exporting and importing photos.)

Another option is to go to the temporary Photos Library in **Finder->Pictures**, right-click on it (or two-finger-click) and choose **Show Package Contents**.

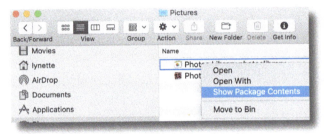

The **Masters** folder that you will see in here contains all the original photos, as downloaded from **iCloud Photos**.

Open your main Photos library in the Photos app, and drag the **Masters** folder you just found onto this window (which triggers an **import** of the **Masters** photos).

If you are asked what to do with duplicates, choose not to import them – check the box **Apply to all duplicates** and choose **Don't import**.

This import process could take quite a while if you have a lot of photos, so be patient.

Once you have all your phones imported to your main Photos library you can then return to Finder -> Pictures and delete the temporary Photos library.

Getting your Photos out of iCloud Photos – Windows

If you have a Windows computer, you can could switch on **iCloud for Windows** to get your photos out of iCloud.

Getting your Photos out of iCloud Photos

Once iCloud for Windows is installed, choose **iCloud Photos** from File Explorer. You will see the **Download photos and videos** option in the navigation bar.

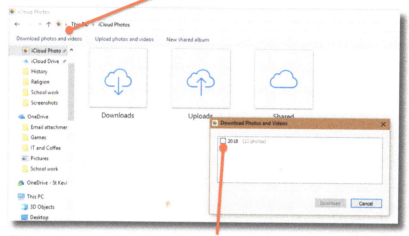

You will have the option to select what years' pictures and videos you want to download to the iCloud Photos Downloads folder.

Tick the years you require and choose the **Download** button to start the process.

Just be warned that it may take some time for the **Download photos and videos** option to become available, as your Windows computer must scan the iCloud Photos contents to work out what is available – before it can show the list of years that are available.

Once you choose the **Download** button (after selecting the required years), your patience will be tested again – as your download of photos could take days and days if you have lots of photos.

As described earlier, this time also depends on the speed of your internet connection.

My Photo Stream

My Photo Stream is part of iCloud – a feature that you can choose to enable on each of your Apple devices.

(***Important Note.*** *If you are using iCloud Photos, you generally won't need to use My Photo Stream - unless you have a device that is not yet using iCloud Photos. In fact, for newer iCloud accounts, the My Photo Stream feature is no longer available as Apple wants you to use iCloud Photos instead.*)

My Photo Stream's purpose is to allow streaming of photos (**not videos**) between your **My Photo Stream**-enabled devices.

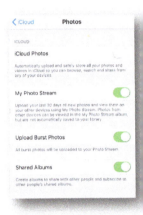

If your iPad or iPhone has this feature turned **on**, photos you take on that device will be uploaded to iCloud for 30 days. A Wi-Fi connection is required for this upload to occur. Any photo you take on your iPhone will appear on your iPad (and vice-versa).

If the feature is turned **on** in your iCloud settings on the Mac, photos found in your iCloud's **My Photo Stream** will automatically download to your Mac when it is connected to the internet.

Your iCloud's **My Photo Stream** photos can also be automatically downloaded to your Windows computer if you have installed **iCloud for Windows**

The **My Photo Stream** album in the **Photos** app on the iPad and iPhone shows the photos that have been downloaded to the device from your iCloud's **My Photo Stream**.

On your iPad and iPhone, the **My Photo Stream** album will only ever hold the last 1000 photos that were downloaded from your iCloud's **My Photo Stream**.

Older photos will disappear from your device's **My Photo Stream** album once 1000 is reached. No such limit applies on the Mac (or on a Windows computer using iCloud for Windows).

(*Important Note. The My Photo Stream album is not present in the Photos app if* **iCloud Photos** *is turned On. In this case, photos downloaded from your iCloud's My Photo Stream will simply appear in the All Photos album and in your Photos timeline.*)

See the earlier description of how to find the **My Photo Stream** in the relevant settings/preferences.

Shared Albums

Share photos with friends and family

iCloud allows the sharing of your photos with other people via a feature in the **Photos** app called **Shared Albums.**

This feature allows you to create an album of photos in your iCloud, that other people can also see via their own **Photos** app, via their web browser or, on Windows, in a particular folder in Pictures.

This shared album can be added to after creation – both by the person who created it, and (optionally) by those with whom it has been shared.

Anyone who you have invited to share your Shared Album can post comments about the photos – these comments are then seen by others who also share that Shared Album.

These Shared Albums do not contribute to your iCloud storage allowance.

Enabling Shared Albums

To be able to use Shared iCloud Albums, you must first turn on this feature in **Settings** on the iPad and iPhone, in **Photos -> Preferences -> iCloud** on the Mac, and in the **iCloud for Windows** settings on Windows.

Make sure the **Shared Albums** setting is switched to **On** (green.)

We won't go into more details about Shared Albums here - refer to the following iTandCoffee guides for full details about sharing photos using Shared Albums.

- Introduction to the Mac – The Photos App (Mojave Edition)
- Introduction to the iPad and iPhone – Managing your Photos and Videos with Photos (iOS 12 Edition)

Visit **itandcoffee.com.au/guides** for more details about these guides.

Solving iCloud Confusion

As mentioned earlier, iCloud is designed to manage, synchronise and share the data for a single person and, in as a general rule, should not be shared by more than one person.

If you find that someone else is using your Apple ID, or that you are using someone else's Apple ID, the device/s using the wrong Apple ID must be detached from that Apple ID by signing out from Settings.

Before you sign out

If the device has been using **iCloud Photos**, you will need to consider what you want to do about the photos that have been going into the other person's iCloud. These photos may disappear from your device when you sign out of iCloud.

If, in **Settings -> [your-name] -> iCloud -> Photos**, the **Download and Keep Originals** option is selected, the photos taken with the device should still be stored on the device, so should not be impacted when that device is signed out of iCloud.

To check if all the photos reside permanently on the device, open the **Photos** app and tap the **Photos** option. Make sure you are looking at the last photo taken.

Underneath that you will see a total count of photos and videos.

If you see a message like that above right – **Downloading n Originals** – then you may want to delay signing out of the device's iCloud until all the remaining photos have been downloaded.

(It could be, however, that the photos awaiting download are those taken by other people who use the same Apple ID for iCloud – and that you will not want to download them to this device.)

If, in **Settings -> [your-name] -> iCloud -> Photos**, the **Optimise iPhone (iPad) Storage** option is selected, then photos may not be stored permanently on the device – and may not be able to be downloaded due to storage space restrictions.

You can try to get them downloaded to the device before turning off iCloud, by choosing the **Download and Keep Originals** option.

Solving iCloud Confusion

When you select that option, you may receive a message advising that there is insufficient space, in which case you will find that photos will disappear from the device when you sign it out of the shared iCloud account.

They will still be available to view via **iCloud.com** – and can be downloaded from there if needed (although you will need a computer for this). The photos could also be Airdropped to the device by the other person who uses that iCloud account. Or they could be shared using a Shared Album, as described above.

If selecting the **Download and Keep Originals** option does not give you a message about lack of space, then you may need to wait a while for the download ot the photos to complete. Keep checking the Photos app (as described above) to see when the download is complete.

Only once this download of photos is complete can you sign out of that iCloud, as described next.

How to sign out of the wrong iCloud

Go to **Settings -> [your-name]**.

The **Sign Out** option is the very last option on that screen.

If the **Find my iPhone** option was enabled, the password for the Apple ID will need to be entered, in order to disable this.

This is a security option, as **Find my iPhone** puts an 'activation lock' on the phone as a theft deterrent.

You will then need to decide whether you want to keep any of the iCloud data from that Apple ID on the device.

Turn to **On** or **Off** the different types of iCloud data that you do or don't want to retain from the iCloud that you have been using.

Solving iCloud Confusion

Even if some of this data belongs to someone else, you can always choose to keep it and then do a cleanup later, once you are 'disconnected'.

Once you have done chosen what data to keep, choose the Sign Out option at top right to complete the process.

You can then sign in with your own Apple ID – creating a new one Apple ID if you don't already have one of your own. See page 24 for further details on how to sign in with your own Apple ID.

If you were using a shared iTunes account

In situations where you have been previously sharing an iCloud AND iTunes account, you may still wish to continue sharing the iTunes and App Store purchases that you previously made with that account – even after you get a separate Apple ID for iCloud.

This is where **Family Sharing** comes in. See earlier in this guide (page 85) for further details of how to set this up so that you can share these purchases.

Other sign outs may be required – Messages & Facetime

If you have been sharing an Apple ID for iCloud, you may also have been sharing this same Apple ID for **Messages** and **Facetime** – perhaps resulting in the wrong person receiving Messages and/or Facetime calls.

Once you have signed out of the shared Apple ID for iCloud purposes, you should also check that the device is signed out of this Apple ID for these other features.

For **Messages**, go to **Settings -> Messages -> Send and Receive**.

If you see an Apple ID in blue at the top and the email address shown there the shared Apple ID, tap on that blue email and then choose the Sign Out option.

Similarly, for **Facetime**, in **Settings -> Facetime**, check if the same Apple ID appears there. If it does, tap on it and choose Sign Out.

In both areas of Settings, then tap the Use your Apple ID for ... option and sign back in with the alternative Apple ID.

Other Guides by iTandCoffee

Introduction to the iPad and iPhone Series

Multiple guides covering topics like

- A Guided Tour
- The Camera App
- The Photos App
- Typing and Editing
- The Mail App
- The Safari App
- The Calendar App
- The Phone App
- The Contacts App
- Getting Apps and other Content
- The iBooks App

Guides on other topics

- Getting Connected
- Keeping kids safe on the iPad and iPhone
- Travelling with your iPad and iPhone
- Bringing your Busy Life Under Control using your iPad and iPhone
- Getting to Know your Mac (Series of 5 Guides)

Visit **itandcoffee.com.au/guides** for more details

CPSIA information can be obtained
at www.ICGtesting.com
Printed in the USA
BVHW061906080920
588351BV00008B/517